SCOTT JOPLIN

SCOTT JOPLIN

◄❀►

Katherine Preston

Senior Consulting Editor
Nathan Irvin Huggins
Director
W.E.B. Du Bois Institute for Afro-American Research
Harvard University

CHELSEA HOUSE PUBLISHERS
New York   Philadelphia

Editor-in-Chief Nancy Toff
Executive Editor Remmel T. Nunn
Managing Editor Karyn Gullen Browne
Copy Chief Juliann Barbato
Picture Editor Adrian G. Allen
Art Director Giannella Garrett
Manufacturing Manager Gerald Levine

Staff for SCOTT JOPLIN
Senior Editor Richard Rennert
Associate Editor Perry King
Assistant Editor Gillian Bucky
Editorial Assistant Laura-Ann Dolce
Copy Editors Michael Goodman, Terrance Dolan
Associate Picture Editor Juliette Dickstein
Picture Researcher Alan Gottlieb
Senior Designer Laurie Jewell
Design Assistant Laura Lang
Production Coordinator Joseph Romano
Cover Illustration Alan J. Nahigian

Creative Director Harold Steinberg

3 5 7 9 8 6 4

Library of Congress Cataloging in Publication Data

Preston, Katherine.
  Scott Joplin.

  (Black Americans of achievement)
  Bibliography: p.
  Includes index.
  1. Joplin, Scott, 1868–1917—Juvenile literature.
2. Composers—United States—Biography—Juvenile
literature. [1. Joplin, Scott, 1868–1917. 2. Composers.
3. Afro-Americans—Biography] I. Title. II. Series.
ML3930.J66P7 1988   780′.92′4 [B] [92]   87-21218
ISBN 1-55546-598-6
    0-7910-0205-5 (pbk.)

CONTENTS

BLACK AMERICANS OF ACHIEVEMENT

MUHAMMAD ALI
heavyweight champion

RICHARD ALLEN
*founder of the
African Methodist
Episcopal church*

LOUIS ARMSTRONG
musician

JAMES BALDWIN
author

BENJAMIN BANNEKER
*scientist and
mathematician*

MARY MCLEOD BETHUNE
educator

BLANCHE K. BRUCE
politician

RALPH BUNCHE
diplomat

GEORGE WASHINGTON CARVER
botanist

CHARLES WADDELL CHESTNUTT
author

PAUL CUFFE
abolitionist

FREDERICK DOUGLASS
abolitionist editor

CHARLES R. DREW
physician

W. E. B. DUBOIS
educator and author

PAUL LAURENCE DUNBAR
poet

DUKE ELLINGTON
bandleader and composer

RALPH ELLISON
author

ELLA FITZGERALD .
singer

MARCUS GARVEY
black-nationalist leader

PRINCE HALL
social reformer

WILLIAM H. HASTIE
educator and politician

MATTHEW A. HENSON
explorer

CHESTER HIMES
author

BILLIE HOLIDAY
singer

JOHN HOPE
educator

LENA HORNE
entertainer

LANGSTON HUGHES
poet

JAMES WELDON JOHNSON
author

MARTIN LUTHER KING, JR.
civil rights leader

SCOTT JOPLIN
composer

JOE LOUIS
heavyweight champion

MALCOLM X
militant black leader

THURGOOD MARSHALL
Supreme Court justice

ELIJAH MUHAMMAD
religious leader

JESSE OWENS
champion athlete

GORDON PARKS
photographer

SIDNEY POITIER
actor

ADAM CLAYTON POWELL, JR.
political leader

A. PHILIP RANDOLPH
labor leader

PAUL ROBESON
singer and actor

JACKIE ROBINSON
baseball great

JOHN RUSSWURM
publisher

SOJOURNER TRUTH
antislavery activist

HARRIET TUBMAN
antislavery activist

NAT TURNER
slave revolt leader

DENMARK VESEY
slave revolt leader

MADAME C. J. WALKER
entrepreneur

BOOKER T. WASHINGTON
educator

WALTER WHITE
political activist

RICHARD WRIGHT
author

ON
ACHIEVEMENT

Coretta Scott King

BEFORE YOU BEGIN this book, I hope you will ask yourself what the word excellence means to you. I think that it's a question we should all ask, and keep asking as we grow older and change. Because the truest answer to it should never change. When you think of excellence, perhaps you think of success at work; or of becoming wealthy; or meeting the right person, getting married, and having a good family life.

Those important goals are worth striving for, but there is a better way to look at excellence. As Martin Luther King, Jr., said in one of his last sermons, "I want you to be first in love. I want you to be first in moral excellence. I want you to be first in generosity. If you want to be important, wonderful. If you want to be great, wonderful. But recognize that he who is greatest among you shall be your servant."

My husband, Martin Luther King, Jr., knew that the true meaning of achievement is service. When I met him, in 1952, he was already ordained as a Baptist preacher and was working toward a doctoral degree at Boston University. I was studying at the New England Conservatory and dreamed of accomplishments in music. We married a year later, and after I graduated the following year we moved to Montgomery, Alabama. We didn't know it then, but our notions of achievement were about to undergo a dramatic change.

You may have read or heard about what happened next. What began with the boycott of a local bus line grew into a national movement, and by the time he was assassinated in 1968 my husband had fashioned a black movement powerful enough to shatter forever the practice of racial segregation. What you may not have read about is where he got his method for resisting injustice without compromising his religious beliefs.

He got the strategy of nonviolence from a man of a different race, who lived in a distant country, and even practiced a different religion. The man was Mahatma Gandhi, the great leader of India, who devoted his life to serving humanity in the spirit of love and nonviolence. It was in these principles that Martin discovered his method for social reform. More than anything else, those two principles were the key to his achievements.

This book is about black Americans who served society through the excellence of their achievements. It forms a part of the rich history of black men and women in America—a history of stunning accomplishments in every field of human endeavor, from literature and art to science, industry, education, diplomacy, athletics, jurisprudence, even polar exploration.

Not all of the people in this history had the same ideals, but I think you will find something that all of them have in common. Like Martin Luther King, Jr., they all decided to become "drum majors" and serve humanity. In that principle—whether it was expressed in books, inventions, or song—they found something outside themselves to use as a goal and a guide. Something that showed them a way to serve others, instead of living only for themselves.

Reading the stories of these courageous men and women not only helps us discover the principles that we will use to guide our own lives, but it teaches us about our black heritage and about America itself. It is crucial for us to know the heroes and heroines of our history and to realize that the price we paid in our struggle for equality in America was dear. But we must also understand that we have gotten as far as we have partly because America's democratic system and ideals made it possible.

We still are struggling with racism and prejudice. But the great men and women in this series are a tribute to the spirit of our democratic ideals and the system in which they have flourished. And that makes their stories special, and worth knowing. ❧

SCOTT
JOPLIN

1

THE MAPLE LEAF CLUB

❧

I T IS A SULTRY summer evening just at the turn of the century in Sedalia, Missouri, a town almost 200 miles west of St. Louis. Most of the residents in this town of 15,000 people have already finished their dinner and have gone outside. Many of them now sit quietly on their front porches, rocking and fanning themselves from the heat, while their neighbors, out for an evening stroll along the tree-lined streets, trade news or gossip with their friends.

Lightning bugs flicker on and off in the grass and bushes. Children are allowed to play one last game of tag before they are called inside. Then the glow of oil and gas lamps brightens the windows of the houses on Sedalia's residential streets as another busy day in this prosperous midwestern town seems to be drawing to a close.

However, the scene that is taking place only a few blocks away—in the vicinity of Main Street—is not quite so sedate. Although all of the daytime business establishments—including the seed stores, the harness shops, and the general stores—are closed until the morning, the streets are far from deserted. Because Sedalia is a stopover for several major railway lines, a lot of railroad employees are out on the town. They will be staying in Sedalia until the following morning, yet they do not seem to mind having to stay there overnight. Sedalia has a reputation as a

Originally published in 1899, "Maple Leaf Rag" was the first of Joplin's ragtime pieces to achieve widespread popularity.

11

A rare photograph of Joplin taken around 1900 shows the gifted composer shortly after he arrived in Sedalia, Missouri.

lively town, and so they are looking forward to an evening of excitement and entertainment.

Groups of young men from the railroad unite with businessmen, gamblers, and women in fancy dress to form a constant swirl of motion. They jostle each other as they crowd the wooden sidewalks and cross the dusty dirt streets, walking past the open doorways of the saloons and brothels. From these doorways drift the sounds of laughter and piano music.

The people who are walking east along Main Street hear a barbershop quartet singing a number of popular songs. The singing, which is not quite in tune but has a lot of spirit, ends amid a burst of applause and shouts of laughter. As the cheers and laughter begin to die down, the sounds of the night are replaced by music being played on an upright piano.

A steady stream of people—both black and white—head in the direction of the music, which is coming from a club located over a feed store at 121 East Main Street. It is called the Maple Leaf Club, and it was founded just two years before, in 1898.

Although membership in the Maple Leaf Club is limited to blacks only, the clientele is integrated. This mixing of the races might strike some visitors to Sedalia as odd, for in most places in turn-of-the-century America, blacks and whites do not mix socially. However, the Maple Leaf Club has developed a reputation as one of *the* places to visit in town. It is especially recommended for people who like the new and still developing form of music called ragtime.

The source of the Maple Leaf Club's lofty reputation is readily obvious as soon as a person climbs the stairs and enters the club. For the official club pianist is none other than Scott Joplin, the indisputable ragtime king.

Despite the summer heat, the club is crowded. It is a large smoky room dominated by mirrors and a huge carved walnut bar. Gas chandeliers swing over-

Ragtime music took the country by storm shortly after the turn of the century. Shown here is a ragtime pianist entertaining a group of ladies at a club in New Orleans, Louisiana.

⇥THE GOOD TIME BOYS.⇤

WILLIAM'S PLACE, for Williams, E. Cook Allie Ellis, Taylor Williams. Will give a good time, for instance Master Scott Joplin, the entertainer. W. J. Williams the slow wonder said that H. L. Dixon, the cracker-jack around ladies said E, Cook, the ladies masher told Dan Smith, the clever boy, he saw L n Williams, the dude, and he said that there are others but not so good. These are the members of the "Maple Leaf Club,". ☞Don't forget Jake Powel, the plunger and King of kitchen machanic.

The owners of the Maple Leaf Club listed "Master Scott Joplin, the entertainer" on their business cards for the purpose of attracting patrons to their club.

head. There are scores of men seated around numerous gaming tables, playing dice or poker. Groups of men also surround large green pool tables. Some of the men hold cue sticks and study the layout, while others bend over the tables, concentrating on their shots, as people chat amiably and the piano plays on.

Seated at the piano, the 31-year-old Joplin seems to be ignoring all of the commotion around him. He occasionally glances up and flashes a smile as someone yells a greeting to him from across the room. But most of the time he is serious and remarkably caught up in his music. Although he is a small, dark man who dresses quietly and neatly, he commands a lot of attention when he is at the piano.

Over the course of the evening at the Maple Leaf Club, Joplin will launch into a rousing piece of music that will have all of the people in the club tapping their feet and clapping their hands. And if he "rags" (playfully changes) a tune that everyone knows, a lot of folks will start to sing along. After this song is over, he might begin to play a brand-new piece. Then again he might improvise a piece as he goes along, playing each verse a little differently from the others but all the while incorporating the syncopated, "ragged" rhythm that is the hallmark of ragtime.

At least several times each night, Joplin will oblige the requests of his audience and play some of his own compositions, including "Maple Leaf Rag," which was probably named for the club. When he plays this piece, which is just beginning to achieve widespread popularity, many of his listeners will start to clap along with the music. Some might even break into an impromptu dance. A number of coins will have been added to Joplin's growing pile of tips by the time he ends his rendition.

The music making continues throughout the night as people come and go. By the early-morning hours, only a few people are left in the room: musicians who have been assembling in the club over the course of the evening. Some of these musicians are visiting friends in Sedalia, others are just passing through town, and the rest are local pianists who play at other clubs in town but are finished with their work for the evening.

When the Maple Leaf Club finally closes its doors for the night, all of these musicians sit down to play with one another. Although Joplin and some of the other pianists have been working all night, they are eager to play when there are a lot of other musicians around to trade musical ideas, play for each other, and invent new ragtime melodies.

With its roots in black American folk music, ragtime was regarded at first by the American public as being low class and improper. Because it was initially played in saloons and brothels, where a tune was often matched with crude or bawdy lyrics, ragtime was not considered to be a very respectable art form. "Take that ragtime out of my house," musician Eubie Blake was told by his mother when he was a boy just learning how to play the piano.

Pianist Eubie Blake played ragtime music early in his career before becoming noted for his musical comedies and popular songs.

The Maple Leaf Club was located on the top floor of this building on East Main Street in Sedalia.

Ragtime was also one of the first forms of music to jazz up traditional tunes. However, this practice of altering standard songs displeased many people as well. James Europe, one of the most popular black composers and bandleaders in Harlem in the early 1900s, went so far as to deny that this musical form even existed. "There never was any such music as ragtime," he maintained.

Yet many of the first ragtime composers, including Joplin, believed that the music captured the charm of the Victorian era and was full of grace. He felt that the lyrics—not the melodies—were responsible for ragtime's unpopularity in many places. He said:

I have often sat in theatres and listened to beautiful ragtime melodies set to almost vulgar words . . . and I have wondered why some composers will continue to make people hate ragtime because the melodies are set to such bad words.

I have often heard people say, after they had heard a ragtime song, "I like the music but I don't like the words.". . .

If someone were to put vulgar words to a strain of one of Beethoven's beautiful symphonies, people would begin saying, "I don't like Beethoven's symphonies." So it is the unwholesome words and not the ragtime melodies that many people hate.

To turn ragtime into a popular and respectable musical form in the 20th century was not an easy task, for it meant taking the music out of the barrooms and brothels and finding an opportunity to play it before a more cultivated audience. To work toward this goal required patience, diligence, and sacrifice.

Well aware of the challenges that were facing him, Scott Joplin was willing to show that he was as determined as he was talented. He wanted the entire country—not just Sedalia—to discover that ragtime was a legitimate form of music . . . and that he was the ragtime king. ◀◈▶

2

THE TEXAS
FRONTIER

— ❦ —

WHEN SCOTT JOPLIN was born in eastern Texas on November 24, 1868, he entered a world that was still reeling from the effects of the Civil War, which had ended just three years before. Although no major battles had been fought in Texas, the Lone Star State was economically and politically devastated by the war, as was most of the American South. The long, hard process of rebuilding the country had barely begun. For all Americans, the Civil War was history; but for Southerners, its aftermath—the Reconstruction era—was grim, everyday reality.

For most of the people living in eastern Texas, life during the postwar period was very difficult. Poverty and illness were rampant. A destroyed political and economic system needed to be rebuilt.

To make Reconstruction even more complicated, a large part of the Southern population was on the move. Thousands of Southerners were abandoning their homes and moving west, seeking to rebuild their shattered lives. Eastern Texas had been settled in the 1840s, but by the time of Scott's birth, the area still remained largely a frontier, with thousands of homeless people either passing through it or attempting to settle in the area.

The living situation in eastern Texas was particularly bad for black Texans, many of whom were illiterate. In most of the South, it had been illegal

Railroad construction crews such as the one shown here helped to expand the American frontier in the 19th century. One of the results of this expansion was the creation of boomtowns such as Texarkana, Texas.

19

Racial tensions often ran high in the South, where Joplin was raised. A Union soldier is shown here protecting a group of blacks from an angry mob after the Civil War.

for slaves to be taught how to read and write. Once the war was over and slaves were given their freedom, they remained an uneducated people continuing to live in abject poverty, at the mercy of unscrupulous and dishonest whites. Many white Southerners, especially those who had fought for the Confederacy during the Civil War, still felt hostile toward blacks. Freedmen (former slaves) supposedly had legal rights under the laws passed during Reconstruction. However, they had almost no control over their local government and local law enforcement, which remained under the control of whites. As a result, the years following the war were a reign of terror for many blacks. During the first eight months of 1868—the year of Scott's birth—there were 379 recorded murders of freedmen by whites in the state of Texas, while there were only 10 recorded murders of whites by blacks.

The Joplin family, like thousands of other black families in eastern Texas, lived and struggled in this hostile world. Scott was born to a young black couple who worked as laborers on a farm near Cave Springs, Texas. His father, Jiles, had been born in slavery but had been freed in the late 1850s, when he was in his late teens. Scott's mother, Florence Givin Joplin, was a freeborn woman from Kentucky.

Because jobs were not plentiful in eastern Texas, many blacks—both former slaves and freeborn—had little choice but to work as laborers or tenant farmers. For the first few years of Scott's life, his parents eked out a living in virtual semislavery as tenant farmers, tilling another man's land in exchange for a roof over their heads and enough food to feed their growing family. Scott was the Joplins' second child. He had an older brother named Monroe and two younger brothers, Robert and Will. He had two sisters as well.

After slavery was abolished, most of the freed slaves remained in the South. Having little or no education, they were compelled to work the fields in an attempt to earn a living.

The Joplins (much like the family shown here) moved several times as Scott's father traveled in search of work.

The Joplins moved several times shortly after Scott's birth—first to Linden, Texas, and then to Jefferson, Texas—in search of better living conditions. But tenant farming was not a profitable way to earn a living, and Scott's father knew that he had to find better work to support his young family. When he heard that the railroad was hiring men in Texarkana—a bustling frontier town located on the Texas-Arkansas border some 30 miles north of Louisiana—he and his family packed up their meager belongings and headed there.

Scott was still a toddler when his family moved to Texarkana. The town was being developed around the junction of two major railroad lines, the Texas and Pacific Railroad and the Cairo and Fulton Line. Legend has it that the railroad surveyor who was sent to choose the site for the junction marked the place with a wooden sign containing three letters from the name of each nearby state: TEX-ARK-ANA. The town had just been founded when the Joplins arrived; it would grow quite rapidly.

Jiles Joplin landed a job as a laborer with the railroad, which meant that at last he could earn a steady income. He and his wife rented a small house in the black section of town.

For the Joplin children, Texarkana was a tremendously exciting place in which to grow up. There was constant activity in the town as new people arrived daily—on foot, on horseback, on mules, or driven in wagons, buggies, and two-wheeled carts. Houses, stores, saloons, gambling halls, offices, stables, and cafés had to be constructed; the sounds of hammers and saws continually filled the air. Cowboys drove herds of cattle through the streets. Land speculators, gunmen, gamblers, and settlers swarmed along the town's wooden sidewalks. All of this was a huge

The westward migration that took place after the Civil War consisted of thousands of families seeking to escape the war-ravaged East.

change from the relative quiet that the family had known back on the farm.

The great amount of activity in Texarkana meant that jobs were available not only with the railroads but also with construction crews. The railroad hired both blacks and whites as laborers, track layers, menders, brakemen, engineers, and mechanics. Most of the newcomers who came to Texarkana were whites who had left their homes in Alabama, Georgia, Mississippi, and the Carolinas. But the promise of work also attracted many blacks. As a result, although Texarkana was predominantly a white community, it had a substantial black population right from the start. The presence of a large black community would prove to be crucial to Scott's musical development, for it would enable him to become familiar with the African and Afro-American rhythms and sounds that would eventually be incorporated into ragtime.

Scott's parents were very interested in their children's education. Although most freedmen were illiterate, they knew that an education represented a possible way out of poverty. However, it was not very easy to obtain an education in the 1870s. The public school system was just being established amid opposition from people who did not want their tax dollars used to pay for the education of other people's children. Opposition to schools for black children was particularly vehement—and often violent. It was not uncommon for the few schools that were set up for blacks in the South to be burned down and for the teachers who taught in these schools to be horsewhipped and run out of town.

There were no schools for blacks in Texarkana in the 1870s. But Scott's parents, like many of their neighbors, arranged for their children to be taught by the literate adults in the black community. So Scott and his brothers and sisters learned to read and write by being tutored rather than by sitting in the classroom of a public school.

The Joplin children were also taught music at an early age. And it quickly became quite obvious that when it came to music, Scott possessed extraordinary ability.

Music making in the home was very popular among Americans during the late 1800s, before the advent of the phonograph. Children learned to play music as a matter of course. The piano and the guitar were among the most popular instruments that they studied. Most homes had a piano, and most families had at least one member who could play it with some skill. When families and friends gathered together, it was not unusual for someone to bring along a stack of sheet music to sing or play. In fact, Americans of all ages in the 19th century eagerly bought and learned the latest piece of sheet music, just as future generations would buy recordings of their favorite songs.

Music was especially popular in the black community of Texarkana, and the Joplin household was no exception. In fact, the Joplins may have been even more musically active than most of their neighbors. Jiles Joplin, who studied the violin when he was a boy, had played in the plantation orchestra for dances held in his master's house when he had been a slave. Florence Joplin played the banjo and also sang. Scott's brothers and sisters all had pleasant voices. However, he could outdo all of them when it came to musical ability.

By the time Scott was seven years old, he had learned how to play the banjo. But it was the piano that fascinated him the most. Although his family did not then own a piano, he was irresistibly drawn to one that belonged to a neighbor.

Jiles Joplin did not want to encourage Scott's interest in music too much, for he believed that it was almost impossible to earn a decent living as a musician. However, Scott's mother was delighted with Scott's musical ability and constantly encouraged him to continue playing. The boy was so obviously mu-

The plucking technique employed by banjo players changed the way that some pianists played their instruments and helped to develop the sounds of ragtime music. Joplin knew how to play the banjo by the time he was seven years old.

sical, in fact, that music teachers in the black community quickly began to notice his talent. Several of them offered to teach him without charging anything for lessons.

Scott's most influential teacher was undoubtedly J. C. Johnson, a mulatto who lived on Wood Street, only a few blocks from the Joplin home. Although Johnson was something of a jack-of-all-trades—he was a barber, real estate trader, and musician—he was best known as a music teacher. The "Professor," as Johnson was often addressed, gave lessons in his home on the piano, violin, and the horn. He was eager to teach Scott, for students of his ability were few and far between, and offered to do so without charging him a fee. Johnson taught Scott how to read music and how to play the piano, and he played for Scott piano arrangements of some of the great instrumental and operatic compositions of Europe, undoubtedly introducing these forms of music to his student.

By the time Scott was 11 years old, he could play written pieces smoothly and skillfully. Perhaps even more impressive was his ability to compose his own music and to improvise while he played.

In 1880, when Scott was 12 years old, his father left home. He had been arguing with his wife for some time. It is possible that some of their arguments had involved Scott. His father was adamant that a musician's life was not practical; he would not allow any of his sons to pursue such a career. However, Scott's mother continued to encourage Scott to develop his musical gift.

After Jiles left the household, he stayed in Texarkana and maintained close contact with the family. But he never lived with them again. Unfortunately, the family's economic situation worsened once he left. Florence became responsible for supporting five children, none of them yet in their teens; Monroe, who was eight years older than Scott, had already left home and was supporting himself in Texarkana. Florence immediately moved the family to cheaper housing on the Arkansas side of Texarkana, where most of the blacks lived. She got a job as a maid working in the homes of white families. Despite the family's hardships, Scott's music lessons continued to be given for free.

While Scott was growing up, he often had to run errands and watch his younger brothers and sisters when their mother was at work. Yet he also found time to climb the sandhills that were near the town, play ball in the streets, and go downtown to watch the trains come into the station. However, music was the chief passion in his life.

Scott practiced whenever he could get his hands on a piano. His mother worked for a family that owned a piano, and she was given permission by them to bring Scott to the house while she was cleaning so he could practice. Eventually, she managed to scrape together enough money to buy him a second-hand upright piano. All of the money that he earned by doing odd jobs was soon spent on sheet music, which usually cost 5 or 10 cents.

Although Scott's father felt that making music was nothing more than a pleasant pastime and was not a way to earn a living, Scott believed that music was a way out of poverty and a way out of Texarkana. He soon earned a reputation in both the black and white communities as a talented young musician. People were particularly impressed with his ability to compose his own music. An old family neighbor would recall many years later that Scott "was smart, especially in music. . . . He did not have to play anybody else's music. He made up his own, and it was beautiful! He just got his music out of the air."

Playing the piano and singing from sheet music were two of the most popular ways for people to entertain themselves before the advent of the phonograph.

When Scott was 16, he formed his first musical group, the Texas Medley Quartette. The group was a vocal ensemble made up of Scott, his brother Will, and two neighborhood boys. Their first engagement was in Clarksville, Texas, a town about 80 miles west of Texarkana. Their performance was a resounding success.

Scott's brother Robert soon joined the group as a fifth member, although they continued to call themselves a quartet. They usually performed as a group in the Texarkana area, but Scott was soon in demand as a solo performer—as a pianist—at dances, club meetings, literary and debating societies, church events, social gatherings, picnics, and family get-togethers. The music he played was the standard popular music of the period: marches, songs from the minstrel stage, arrangements of operatic arias, tunes from the theater, church music, early blues songs, sentimental ballads, and popular sheet music. Sometimes he would play them as written; sometimes he would change them, jazzing them up with the more complicated and intricate rhythms that were part of the African musical heritage of the black community. Sometimes he even played tunes that he made up as he went along.

Scott's determination to succeed as a musician may have stemmed in part from his lack of inviting alternatives. For a young black man in Texarkana in the 1880s, there were few career opportunities. Available jobs fell into two categories: He could be either a manual laborer for the railroad, the sawmill, or the lumber camp, or he could be a servant in a white household. Manual labor never appealed to Scott, and his pride would not allow him to work as another man's servant. Besides, he knew that his musical ability gave him an option that most of his peers did not have, and he was determined to make the most of this opportunity.

More than anything else, Scott was stubborn, determined, ambitious, and hardworking. A former neighbor would later say of him, "Scott was earnest. When a bunch of boys got together on a spree one night and asked Scott to go with them, he said, 'No sir, I won't have anything to do with such foolishness. I'm going to make a man out of myself.' "

By the time Scott was in his late teens, he had achieved a great deal of success as a musician in his hometown. He probably would have made a comfortable and fairly secure living by performing and teaching had he remained in Texarkana. However, he had seen a little of the world when he had traveled with the Texas Medley Quartette, and he wanted to see more. He knew that his ability was special, and he was wise enough to know that being a big fish in the small pond of Texarkana ultimately would not satisfy him. So, in 1888, when he was 20 years old, he packed his bags and left home for good. ❧

3

ON THE ROAD

❧

IN THE LATE 1880s, much of the Midwest was still a frontier. When the federal government opened up the Oklahoma Territory to homesteaders in 1889, an astonishing number of settlers streamed to the area from other parts of the country. Oklahoma City, for example, went from a population of zero to 10,000 on April 22, 1889—the day that settlement began in the Oklahoma Territory.

One of the greatest mass migrations in the history of mankind, the westward expansion had a great impact on the lives of the people in the midwestern part of the United States. To some of them, it seemed as if the entire country was on the move as people gave up their homes in the older, more settled parts of the East and headed west. Traveling however they could—by riding mules and horses, driving teams of oxen hitched to wagons, riding on steamboats and in railroad cars—all were lured by the promise of free or inexpensive land and the chance to start over and get ahead.

In addition to the influx of settlers, there were also thousands of other itinerants traveling across the countryside: businessmen, land speculators, fortune hunters, and entertainers. Traveling among them were hundreds of musicians who wandered from town to

The growing Midwest was the perfect place for an itinerant musician such as Joplin to settle in the late 1880s.

town. Some had classical training; others could play their instruments by ear only. Some were young; others were old. Some were Europeans who had come to the United States to seek their fortunes; others were homegrown Americans. Many were white; and some were black. A number of these musicians went from town to town, sometimes joining up with a traveling theatrical troupe or a minstrel show, sometimes with another musician or two. Otherwise, they traveled alone.

When a musician arrived at a new town in the late 1880s, it was relatively easy for him—especially if he was a skilled and reliable pianist—to find a job. The piano was then the most popular instrument with an American public anxious to hear live music making. Jobs for pianists were often available in saloons, restaurants, pool halls, stores, and theaters. Musicians were also hired to play on steamboats, at parties, dances, picnics, horse races, and county fairs.

Although playing in a saloon or bordello was not considered to be socially acceptable, such a job could be an exciting one for a young musician like Joplin. He traveled around the countryside for some time, probably stopping in Texas, Louisiana, Kansas, Oklahoma, Missouri, Arkansas, and Illinois. Sometime around 1890, he surfaced in St. Louis, Missouri. Regarded as the gateway to the West, St. Louis was then one of the major staging points for people heading out to the frontier. Because the city was a temporary refuge to a lot of people, it developed the reputation as a wide-open town, filled with travelers on the move.

St. Louis is located on the brown, wide, and powerful Mississippi River, which was home to all kinds of vessels, including majestic paddle-wheel steamboats. The city had a well-known nightlife area featuring cafés, saloons, boardinghouses, and brothels. This area, which was called Chestnut Valley because one of its boundaries included Chestnut Street, was considered to be the underside of St. Louis—the neighborhood that respectable people did not visit, even though they knew it existed. Rich cattlemen, businessmen, and fancily dressed travelers with money to spend were among those who went to Chestnut Valley for entertainment. Musicians from all over the Midwest were also drawn to Chestnut Valley, for there was money to be made and work to be had.

Shortly after Joplin arrived in St. Louis, he went almost immediately to the Silver Dollar Saloon, located at 425 South 12th Street, in the heart of Chestnut Valley. The saloon was owned and operated by "Honest" John Turpin, a black pianist, and his three sons: Robert, Charles, and Thomas. The Silver Dollar Saloon was the gathering place for many musicians, who would meet there after their jobs elsewhere were finished for the evening.

If Joplin was concerned about how he would fare playing the piano in front of his fellow musicians at the Silver Dollar Saloon, he need not have worried. The serious 22 year old from Texarkana immediately won the respect and admiration of the Silver Dollar regulars—many of whom were older and much more experienced than he was. Joplin's piano playing was lyrical and beautiful. And he could compose his own pieces as well as improvise on the spot. Such ability impressed his fellow musicians and left them applauding loudly and enthusiastically.

Joplin quickly became close friends with all of the Turpins. He found an especially kindred spirit in Tom Turpin. Like Joplin, he was a composer and a pianist, and he wanted to pursue a career as a musician.

Joplin and Tom Turpin made an interesting pair. Turpin was large and burly, while Joplin was slightly built. Joplin was also very quiet; he rarely spoke above a whisper. And he was plain and neat in his dress—unlike many of the people who performed in saloons

Minstrel shows were first performed by whites who spread burnt cork on their faces so as to appear black, then parodied the behavior of blacks during their shows.

One of Joplin's closest friends, Tom Turpin (shown here) became the first black composer to have a rag published when his "Harlem Rag" was released in 1897.

and wore loud outfits, which might consist of a checkered suit, bright silk shirt, and a patterned tie.

Joplin kept a low profile in St. Louis, much like when he was a boy who refused to take part in a spree with his friends. He was serious about his music and was determined to succeed in his chosen profession. He performed in saloons and honky-tonks not because he enjoyed the atmosphere but because they were places where he could find work.

Because of Joplin's early success at the Silver Dollar, he was able to land jobs at other establishments in Chestnut Valley as well as elsewhere in St. Louis. For the next few years, he lived with the Turpins and used St. Louis as his base of operations, traveling to other Missouri towns, such as Hannibal, Carthage, Columbia, and Sedalia. He also went to more distant cities, such as Cincinnati, Ohio, and Louisville, Kentucky.

Throughout this period in his life, Joplin constantly worked on developing his own style of piano playing while listening to the songs and styles of other pianists. He gave little thought to writing down his own compositions and trying to get them published, even though he was urged to do so by his friends. He believed that his chances of getting published were so slim that it was hardly worth the effort to try. Not only was he a black musician existing on the fringes of society, but the music that he played and wrote was not considered to be very respectable. Ragtime was associated with the kinds of places that upstanding people did not patronize. However, society's view of this form of music would soon change.

The musicians whom Joplin met in his travels came from different racial, cultural, and educational backgrounds. As they listened to each other, they compared notes, traded tunes, and borrowed melodies, rhythms, and techniques. The results of their interaction were fascinating. A gospel tune might be

combined with a melody from the musical theater, with part of a ballad thrown in for good measure. A classical composition might be mixed into a song from a minstrel show. An operatic aria might be combined with a march by John Philip Sousa, whose work was then extremely popular. Civil War ballads, country dances, jigs and reels, plantation melodies, work songs, classical pieces—all types of music were used and they were all mixed together.

Of overriding importance in this mixing of sounds was rhythm. The complex rhythms of African music, which had been preserved by slaves in their work songs and chants, in their spiritual tunes and banjo playing, became the distinguishing characteristics of the new music that was evolving. More intricate than

Bandmaster John Philip Sousa (shown holding a baton) is best known for having composed many popular marches. However, his bands also played syncopated music well before the rise of ragtime.

West African drum bands developed the syncopated sounds that were eventually used in ragtime music.

the rhythms that were generally used by most composers of classical music, these complex African-based rhythms did not sound very smooth to the average listener. They sounded ragged and made the music seem as though it had "ragged time." The term that eventually evolved to describe this music was *ragtime*.

In 1893, Joplin and some of his St. Louis musician friends went to Chicago to look for work at the Chicago World's Columbian Exposition, a huge world's fair. It was called the Columbian Exposition because it was a celebration of the 400th anniversary of Christopher Columbus's discovery of the New World. This visit to Chicago and the fair marked a turning point in Joplin's career. While he was there, he met many other musicians from all over the country who were also experimenting with ragtime music. Also important was his exposure at the fair to black music and black musicians who performed before white audiences and were treated with respect. For the first time, he realized that it was possible for black music and black musicians to be treated with respect throughout American society.

While Joplin was in Chicago, he formed a band consisting (most likely) of a cornet, clarinet, tuba, and baritone horn. He arranged pieces for the band, and they performed whenever they could find employment around the fairgrounds or in Chicago's red-light district. His work with the band gave him the opportunity to try his hand at writing out the musical parts in a composition for each of the various instruments. This experience would prove to be quite valuable once he began to work on his own compositions.

Among the many musicians whom Joplin met while he was in Chicago was Otis Saunders, a 22-year-old pianist and composer who was visiting the

The World Columbian Exposition, which was held in Chicago in 1893, enabled Joplin to meet musicians from all over the country.

At the turn of the century, brass bands were a popular entertainment attraction at picnics and other large outings. An accomplished cornet player as well as a gifted pianist, Joplin occasionally played at such events.

fair from his home in Springfield, Missouri. Saunders was impressed with Joplin's music and urged him to try to get some of his compositions published. Saunders soon became an important friend of Joplin's.

In 1894, Joplin and Saunders left Chicago together and traveled slowly back to St. Louis, stopping frequently on the way to perform at different places. They arrived in St. Louis sometime near the start of 1895 and stayed with the Turpins. Tom Turpin told Joplin that he had decided to try to sell some of his musical compositions. Joplin, heartened by what he had seen in Chicago and by his friends' encouragement, was also beginning to think that he should try to get his work published.

Joplin and Saunders did not stay with the Turpins for very long. They soon moved on to Sedalia, where they were joined by two of Joplin's brothers, Will and Robert. Both of them were proficient musicians. Robert, who was 26 years old, sang and played the violin and guitar. Will, who was 19 years old, sang, played several instruments, and did a little composing. Joplin had kept in contact with his brothers while he traveled around the country. Encouraged by his success as a musician, they both wanted to pursue a musical career with their older brother's help.

Soon after Will and Robert arrived in Sedalia, Joplin revived the Texas Medley Quartette. This time the group was a double quartet, featuring eight sing-

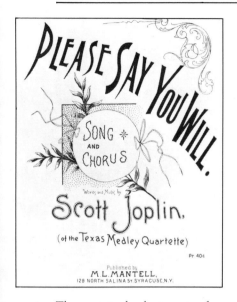

The cover to the sheet music of "Please Say You Will," one of the first songs that Joplin had published.

ers. After several rehearsals, the group went on the road. They were successful enough to attract a management agency, the Majestic Booking Agency, which arranged their tours. The group's first trip took them as far east as Syracuse, New York. In 1895 and 1896, the group toured all over Missouri, Texas, Oklahoma, and Kansas, performing medleys of popular songs and plantation tunes such as Stephen Foster's "Old Folks at Home," "My Old Kentucky Home," and "Camptown Races." They also performed songs that Joplin had written.

Because Joplin had to teach his songs to the members of the Texas Medley Quartette, he found that the easiest way to achieve this was for him to write down the songs. Once he had the songs on paper, he remembered the encouragement he was given by Saunders, who was accompanying the group on their tour, and from Tom Turpin. Toward the end of 1895, when the group was performing in Syracuse, he approached some local publishers with his songs. Two of his compositions—sentimental songs written in a popular style—were accepted. M. L. Mantell published "Please Say You Will," and the Lieter Brothers published the following song, "A Picture of Her Face":

This life is very sad to me, a sorrow fills my heart,
My story I will tell you, from me my love did part,
The village church bell sadly tolled, the one I loved had
    died,
She was a treasure more than gold, when she was by my
    side,
But now she's gone beyond recall, in a silent tomb she
    sleeps,
The one I loved yet most of all has left me here to weep;
Though death so ruthless stole my love, my dear and only
    Grace,
I've yet a treasure in this world, a picture of her face.
(Refrain)
It brings joy to me when ofttimes sad at heart,
Her picture I can see, and sad thoughts then depart;
Although my love is dead, my only darling Grace,
My eyes are ofttimes looking on a picture of her face.

Encouraged by the acceptance of these songs, which were issued in sheet music identifying the composer as a member of the Texas Medley Quartette, Joplin decided to put onto paper more of the many pieces he had already composed. In 1896, he had three more works published in Texas. These three compositions were not songs with lyrics but instrumental pieces written for the piano. They were a waltz and two marches.

All five of Joplin's earliest published compositions were standard works of the period. None of them achieved a great deal of success, nor did any of them give a hint of what was to come. However, these five compositions were a very encouraging start for the young composer, who was about to trade his life on the road for a more stable life-style.

The Texas Medley Quartette ended its final tour in Joplin, Missouri, in 1897 and then disbanded. Joplin then headed back with Saunders to Sedalia, where a fairly settled way of life would help him to concentrate on his ragtime music. ✺

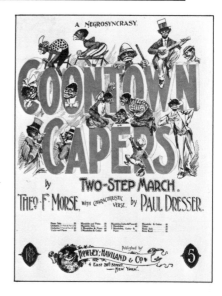

A forerunner of ragtime music, songs such as "Coontown Capers" contained lyrics that offered a comic portrayal of black life and were accompanied by syncopated rhythms.

4

SUCCESS IN
SEDALIA

SEDALIA, MISSOURI, was a logical place for
Joplin to settle down in 1897. The town had a large
and prosperous black community. In fact, the black
community in Sedalia was sizable enough to boast of
having several black newspapers and a college, the
George R. Smith College for Negroes. And like Joplin's hometown of Texarkana, Sedalia was a busy
railroad town, with travelers stopping there quite often.
Consequently, it had developed one of the largest
nightlife districts in the state.

When Joplin moved to Sedalia in 1897, his brothers Will and Robert did not go with him. But even
though he did not have any family in Sedalia, he did
have a large group of friends who were living there.
An old acquaintance who said that Joplin made friends
easily remembered that he "was always accompanied
by a few of his cronies when he strolled about the
streets, or idled on a corner." His friends included
the musicians Arthur Marshall and Scott Hayden,
both of whom were local residents, and Tom Turpin,
who occasionally came to Sedalia to visit Joplin. Yet
Joplin's closest friend in Sedalia continued to be
Saunders. "If one were seen the other wouldn't be
far off," a fellow resident recalled.

Although Joplin was a published composer, he
did not receive much money for his compositions. A
publisher generally bought a composition from a com-

*Bert Williams and George
Walker, a popular black minstrel
team, often entertained their audiences by performing cakewalks to
the accompaniment of ragtime
music.*

A classmate of Joplin's at the Smith College of Music in Sedalia, Arthur Marshall (shown here) often received music lessons and advice about his ragtime compositions from Joplin.

poser for a fee of 25 to 50 dollars. There were no royalties paid to the composer for each piece of his music that was sold, so the publisher would get to pocket all of the profits—if there were any. Accordingly, Joplin came to Sedalia pretty much penniless—simply another black musician in search of work. Neither his economic situation nor his general outlook had changed much during his years of touring. He was still a serious young musician dedicated to his work and his art.

Joplin's desire to have his work published began to grow when a Chicago publisher released the first piece of true ragtime sheet music in 1897. The piece was called the "Mississippi Rag," and it was written by the Chicago bandleader William H. Krell. Now that the first rag had finally made it into print, Joplin was tempted to write down some of his own ragtime music. After all, he could compose ragtime pieces at the drop of a hat. However, he sometimes found that putting the notes on paper was time-consuming and difficult. Making up the tunes was no problem at all; it was a lot more difficult for him to translate music into notes on a page.

Joplin mentioned this problem to Tony Williams, who owned a tavern where the young musician was working. Williams suggested that the best way to learn how to translate music into notes might be for him to study music at the Smith College of Music, which was part of the local black college. This suggestion seemed like a good idea to Joplin, and Saunders agreed with him. So Joplin enrolled in the school, which was located in the suburbs of Sedalia. There he took piano lessons and studied music theory and composition while holding down his job at Williams's tavern in the evenings. His skill at music reading and notation increased rapidly.

Because Joplin had to pay for his college tuition, he expanded his money-earning activities. One of

the former members of the Texas Medley Quartette, Emmett Cook, was a member of an excellent local band called the Sedalia Queen City Concert Band. Joplin was a good cornet player, so Cook helped him to get a position in the 12-piece band. The Queen City Concert Band was the best of several black brass bands in Sedalia at the time. In fact, it may have been one of the best bands in the region, for the ensemble regularly walked away with the prize when it entered band contests around Missouri. Joplin made arrangements of popular tunes so that the band could play them in ragtime. This made the Queen City Concert Band one of the first bands in the area to play ragtime.

The Queen City Concert Band was one of the first bands to play ragtime music. The band is shown here in 1896, the year before Joplin joined the group.

Joplin also formed a smaller, five-piece band—consisting of a cornet, clarinet, baritone horn, tuba, and piano—to play at parties, dances, socials, and get-togethers in Sedalia's black community. In addition, he sang in quartets and played solo piano at social gatherings. These performances were considered to be much more respectable work than playing in a saloon in a red-light district. However, the money that Joplin earned from these more respectable jobs was not enough to support him. So he also continued to work on a regular basis in saloons. He had little trouble moving back and forth between the two kinds of jobs. For him, music was music. It did not matter to him whether his audience was made up of gamblers or socialites.

Cakewalk dances such as the one shown here became extremely popular throughout America in the mid-1890s. Cakewalks were often danced to ragtime music.

While Joplin was establishing his reputation in Sedalia, ragtime was beginning to gain acceptance throughout the country. Although bands were still playing marches as well as other popular kinds of music, the jaunty, syncopated rhythm that is the hallmark of ragtime was beginning to creep into their renditions. In addition, more and more ragtime sheet music was showing up on the racks and in the windows of music stores. It was getting so a person could walk down any residential street in Sedalia—or in almost any other small town in America—and hear strains of ragtime being played on a piano in a house across the lawn. People everywhere were propping up ragtime sheet music on their parlor pianos and struggling to learn its tricky rhythms.

An important element in ragtime's rise in acceptance was the popularity of a ragtimelike dance, the cakewalk. Before this dance became popular, one of the dances performed most often in the 1890s was called the two-step, which was danced in couples, like a waltz. The two-step was basically a glorified march; it was danced to such marches as Sousa's "Washington Post March" and "Stars and Stripes Forever." When dance bands and orchestras started to jazz up their march performances with the jauntier rhythms of ragtime, the dancers discovered that this jazzed-up music did not effect their dancing, for they could still hear the steady march beat under the new and complex rhythm.

The cakewalk, which became popular in the mid-1890s, was a different kind of dance. It was also danced in couples, yet it featured high-stepping, prancing, and strutting. Like ragtime music, it had been in existence for quite a while. The dance form had originated among black slaves in the early part of the century. It may have originally been a parody of the behavior of whites who lived in plantation mansions.

The first rag ever published was "The Mississippi Rag" in 1897. It was written by William Krell, a Chicago bandleader who heard ragtime being played while his group was touring the Midwest.

The publication of Tom Turpin's "Harlem Rag" in 1897 undoubtedly inspired Joplin to publish his own works and thereby helped to launch the ragtime era.

The word *cakewalk* comes from the contests held for performers of this dance. During such contests, the most skilled "walkers" competed for prizes, which sometimes included cakes. In the middle of the 19th century, the cakewalk was featured extensively on the minstrel stage. People from the middle class suddenly discovered the dance in the mid-1890s, and the cakewalk became an overnight sensation.

Ragtime music was the perfect accompaniment to the cakewalk, for the dance is not a set routine. Cakewalk dancers are supposed to improvise steps, struts, and kicks to fit the syncopation of the music.

By 1898, cakewalk contests were being held regularly all across the country as a part of social outings, especially on excursions and picnics. Sedalia was a popular destination for people from the small towns in central Missouri who would go on outings. They would come into Sedalia on one of the railroad lines and have a big picnic in a park. There would be plates of fried chicken, bowls of potato salad, home-grown tomatoes, and watermelon. Along with the eating, there would be exercises, drills, games, cakewalk contests, and maybe even a ragtime competition. And there were dances. Arthur Marshall said, "Joplin and I and many of the others played for numerous dances at the parks, all piano only. We played all the rags of note and they did dances to the ragtime."

Along with his school studies and performances, Joplin continued to write new pieces and attempt to get them published. In late 1897, he persuaded a Kansas City publisher to accept a tune called "Original Rags," although the publisher did not release the composition until 1899. So instead of becoming the first black composer to have a rag published, Joplin saw his friend Tom Turpin attain this honor when his "Harlem Rag" was released in December 1897.

The publication of Turpin's work undoubtedly gave Joplin even more incentive to have his own work published. He finished the first draft of a promising piece called "Maple Leaf Rag" and took it to several publishers in Kansas City and Sedalia, including A. W. Perry & Son. To his great disappointment, the piece was turned down. However, he kept on playing it in various clubs and saloons, polishing it with every performance. Other ragtime pianists also began to play it, and the piece soon started to become quite well known in the area.

"Original Rags" was finally released in early 1899, but because Joplin had sold the work to its publisher almost two years earlier and had been writing new compositions since then, it was not a good example of his best work by the time it was released. His newer compositions—especially "Maple Leaf Rag"—were much more sophisticated and melodious than "Original Rags."

In addition to working on "Maple Leaf Rag," Joplin also collaborated with Hayden and Marshall on two other new works: "Swipsey—Cakewalk" and "Sunflower Slow Drag—a Ragtime Two-Step." When "Sunflower" was finished, Joplin decided that it was time for him to visit another publisher. In August, he took his two best pieces, "Maple Leaf Rag" and "Sunflower," and headed downtown to the publishing firm of John Stark & Son.

Joplin was aware that the danceability of a ragtime piece was a major selling point. So when he went downtown to visit John Stark, he took along with him a little boy who was a good dancer—to demonstrate how very danceable his music was. After Joplin introduced himself to Stark, who was about 45 years old, with a rounded beard, a heavy mustache, and piercing blue eyes, the quiet black composer sat down at the piano and skillfully launched into his

Like many ragtime pieces, Joplin's "Swipesy—Cakewalk" received its title in an offhand way: Publisher John Stark thought that the boy on the cover looked as though he had just swiped some cookies.

When John Stark (shown here) agreed to publish "Maple Leaf Rag" in 1899, he began a business association with Joplin that would last for more than 10 years.

rag. The little boy immediately began to dance to the music. When Joplin finished his first piece, he played the other. The entire performance so impressed Stark that he decided on the spot to publish "Maple Leaf Rag."

Joplin and Stark signed a contract that sealed the agreement. The composer received no money right away, but he was to get a royalty of one cent for each piece of sheet music (priced at 50 cents) that was sold. As it turned out, Stark struck one of the bargains of the century, for sales of "Maple Leaf Rag" eventually made him a relatively wealthy man. Yet Joplin was so eager to have his music published that he probably would have agreed to a contract at almost any terms. And no one—including Stark and Joplin—could have known that the work would eventually become so successful. Also in Stark's defense, few publishers in the early years of ragtime were willing to accept compositions from black composers, so in this respect Stark was a pioneer. He would be well regarded by most black ragtime composers for the rest of his life, for he was one of the few publishers who was willing to give them a chance.

On the cover of the original version of "Maple Leaf Rag," which was first published in September 1899, is an illustration of two black couples dressed in their finery, presumably on their way to a cakewalk dance—an indication of how closely tied ragtime was to the cakewalk fad. The sheet music sold almost 400 copies during its first year in print, which netted Joplin four dollars in royalties. But by the fall of 1900, the piece became extremely popular. Thousands of orders suddenly came pouring into the offices of John Stark & Son, many of them from the F. W. Woolworth chain of stores around the country. The Starks were not able to fill the orders quickly enough. The company, which was small and family run, stopped publication of all of its orders except for "Maple Leaf Rag" and concentrated on churning out as many copies of the piece as possible. Yet the orders continued to come in.

Ragtime music was taking the country by storm, and publishers from all over sought to print anything that they could pass off as the new music. Even old pieces that did not have a hint of ragtime syncopation were rereleased, with new covers containing the magic legend RAGTIME! across the front. However, only a few publishers were printing real rags, and only Stark had the rights to Joplin's "Maple Leaf Rag."

Joplin suddenly became something of a celebrity. He became known in Sedalia as "The King of Rag-

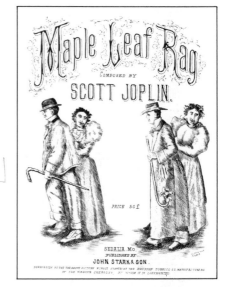

This was the original cover to the sheet music for "Maple Leaf Rag," which became wildly popular in 1900, the year after the rag was first published.

Scott Hayden (shown here) collaborated with Joplin on several ragtime pieces, including "Sunflower Slow Drag."

time," and he played regularly at the Maple Leaf Club, where his nickname was "The Entertainer." (He eventually used this nickname as the title of one of his rags.) Pianists from all over Missouri came to town to compete against him in ragtime contests, which Joplin would invariably win. The winner of a ragtime contest was decided by the audience present at the competition, so even when other pianists brought their own cheering sections to Sedalia, Joplin's fans would easily outnumber and outapplaud them. Along with performing in Sedalia, he continued to give a few performances on the road. In some of the towns in which he appeared, Maple Leaf Clubs were formed in his honor.

The turn of the century marked a happy time for the serious young composer—especially in his personal life, for he fell in love with Belle Hayden, Scott Hayden's younger sister. The musical collaboration between Joplin and Hayden that produced "Sunflower" had given Joplin an excellent opportunity to spend a great deal of time in the Hayden household and to get to know Belle. By late 1900, it was clear that although Belle did not share his passion for music, she loved him. They married shortly thereafter.

Late in 1900, Joplin met a man from St. Louis who would have a profound and far-reaching effect on his life. Alfred Ernst, the German-born director of the St. Louis Choral Symphony Society, visited Sedalia and got to know the 32-year-old ragtime composer. Ernst was quite taken with Joplin and his music. In an interview published by the *St. Louis Post-Dispatch* in February 1901, Ernst said of him:

> I am deeply interested in this man. He is young and undoubtedly has a fine future. With proper cultivation, I believe, his talent will develop into positive genius. Being of African blood himself, Joplin has a keener insight into that peculiar branch of melody than white composers. His ear is particularly acute. . . . The work

Joplin has done in ragtime is so original, so distinctly individual, and so melodious withal, that I am led to believe he can do something fine in compositions of a higher class when he shall have been instructed in theory and harmony. . . . The soul of a composer is there [in Joplin's work] and needs but to be set free by knowledge of techniques. He is an unusually intelligent young man and fairly well educated.

Such words from a European-trained classical musician were music to Joplin's ears. They were also an encouragement to a young composer whose principal desire was to have his music taken seriously. Ernst offered to take on Joplin as a pupil, and he agreed. In early 1901, he and his wife moved to St. Louis, where Ernst lived. While Joplin's head was filled with music, he was also brimming with hopes and plans for the future. ❧

5

THE
KING OF
RAGTIME

❦

T HE RAILROAD TOWN of Sedalia might have felt like home in many ways to Joplin, but his move to St. Louis in 1901 proved to be even more of a homecoming. His brother Robert was living in the city, and within the year their brother Will joined them there as well. Also in St. Louis were Joplin's old friends the Turpins.

John Turpin had yet another saloon, whereas Tom, the proud composer of two published rags, was struggling to make it as a musician. He managed to earn a living by taking on menial jobs and serving as a teacher to a circle of promising young composers and performers.

When Joplin moved back to St. Louis in early 1901, it seemed as though he took a large part of Sedalia's ragtime community with him. Belle's brother, Scott Hayden, who had recently married, soon arrived in St. Louis with his wife and moved into the same row of houses as the Joplins. And other Sedalia musicians—including Otis Saunders, who was touring with McCabe's Minstrel Troupe as a singer, and Arthur Marshall—visited Joplin frequently. Both Hayden and Marshall were appreciably younger than Joplin, and they considered him something of a mentor.

Bars such as this one in Chestnut Valley, the popular red-light district in St. Louis, employed a number of ragtime musicians.

Due mainly to the popularity of "Maple Leaf Rag," Joplin's reputation was beginning to grow by the time he moved to St. Louis in 1901.

Joplin listed himself in the St. Louis city directory simply as "Joplin, Scott, music." He cut back drastically on his performing and tried to concentrate on composing and teaching. That he had become a married man probably had something to do with his decision to spend more time working at home. His growing reputation as a composer and the encouragement he was receiving from Ernst to think of himself as a composer were also responsible for his decision to focus his energies on composing. Instead of working in saloons, he devoted most of his time to what he really wanted to do: study with Ernst and compose.

At the same time that Joplin was attempting to withdraw from the life of a performer, the ragtime craze was reaching new heights of popularity. The Starks' company in Sedalia had finally caught up with the huge backlog of orders of "Maple Leaf Rag." John Stark and his son, Will, were then able to turn their attention to several other Joplin compositions that they had agreed to publish, including his collaboration with Hayden, "Sunflower Slow Drag."

Because the piano was the most popular musical instrument in America, music that was written primarily for the piano—as was ragtime—was virtually guaranteed to be a financial success once it caught on. However, there was one major problem with ragtime pieces for the piano: they were much more difficult to play than the standard popular piece of sheet music. The tricky ragtime rhythm was the stumbling block. In ragtime, there is always a steady beat in the bass, which is played by the pianist with his left hand. The right hand plays the melody. The strong accents in the melody are placed so that they deliberately fall on the weak beats established by the steady rhythm of the left hand. This rhythm technique is known as syncopation; the parts of the melody that are stressed fall in places where one normally does not hear an accented sound. And it is precisely this juxtaposition

of the right-hand melody (with its "wrong" accents) against the steady beat played by the left hand that creates the "ragged time."

Over the years, syncopated rhythms have become common in jazz and rock music, which are in part outgrowths of ragtime. Yet prior to the advent of ragtime, there was very little popular music in the United States that incorporated such complex rhythms. To American listeners and piano players at the turn of the century, ragtime's rhythms were entirely new, somewhat mysterious, and devilishly hard to master.

The arrangers who worked for the major New York music publishers, who printed much of the country's sheet music, also had trouble at first determining how to write down the complex rhythms they heard when ragtime performers played their music. However, as the public began to clamor for ragtime music, these arrangers managed to figure out how to

Joplin lived with his first wife, Belle, in this building in St. Louis, where he spent much of his time studying music and composing.

This advertisement from 1905 features a player piano, which mechanically plays songs that have been recorded on long scrolls. Player pianos made it possible for ragtime to be played in the homes of people who could not master the music's tricky rhythms.

write down the rags. Publishers also hired ragtime composers and performers to write simple pieces so that lesser-skilled piano players could play the music. Because these pieces were playable, they sold well, thus fueling the ragtime craze even more. The commercial musical establishment was soon cranking out hundreds of ragtime compositions. Because the upright pianos in the publishers showrooms had a basically tinny sound, the area in New York where most of the ragtime publishers were based soon became known as Tin Pan Alley.

Although Joplin's rags were not simplified, the demand for them continued as well. To combat the commercialization of ragtime, he deliberately wrote rags that were of a more serious nature and that were to be played slower than the mass-produced rags. This did not seem to hurt his popularity, however. In fact, between 1901 and 1903 he had 16 pieces published. They were "Peacherine Rag," "Augustan Club Waltz," "The Easy Winners," "Cleopha," "A Breeze from Alabama," "Elite Syncopations," "March Majestic," "The Strenuous Life," "Weeping Willow," "Palm Leaf Rag," "I Am Thinking of My Pickaninny Days," "Little Black Baby," "The Ragtime Dance," "Something Doing," "Sunflower Slow Drag," and "The Entertainer."

Joplin used the same formula for most of his rags. "The Entertainer," which today is probably his best-known piece, offers a good example of his work. It starts off with a brief introduction, which is followed by the first section (called the chorus), consisting of an upbeat melody. The second section is in the same key but has a different melody, which is something of an elaboration of the melody of the chorus but often is more complex and exciting. After this, the first section (chorus) is played again. For the third section, the composition changes to another key and introduces a third melody. This is followed by a short

First published in 1902, "The Entertainer" became one of Joplin's best-known rags. In 1973, shortly after it was renamed "The Sting" (and became the theme for the Academy Award-winning movie of the same title), it became a best-selling record.

Written by Irving Berlin in 1911, "Alexander's Ragtime Band" was one of the many highly popular—although musically simple—songs that were issued by New York City's Tin Pan Alley publishers to capitalize on the ragtime sound.

four-measure "bridge," which serves as a transition from the key of the third section back to the original key. The final section, which is played in the original key, has a closing melody that brings the piece to its conclusion.

All of Joplin's rags are sectional. Like "The Entertainer," they have several distinct segments, with each segment having a different melody. A performer usually plays each melody twice before moving on to the next section. The opening melody, or chorus, is almost always repeated after one or two of the new melodies are played.

Joplin signed a five-year contract with John Stark & Son just after "Maple Leaf Rag" became a big hit. The agreement ensured that the Sedalia publisher would have first choice when it came to publishing Joplin's works. It was an extraordinary business arrangement between a white publisher and black composer, especially for around the turn of the century.

Joplin generally kept to his agreement with Stark. However, there were times during the five-year period when the composer had disagreements with Stark, believing that the publisher was not treating him fairly. When such feelings surfaced, Joplin took his work to another publisher—perhaps to show Stark that he did not have complete control over him.

For the most part, Joplin's working arrangement with Stark was harmonious and beneficial to both parties. The majority of their disagreements stemmed from Joplin's intense desire to be considered a serious composer. He was interested in elevating ragtime from the realm of popular music to the realm of serious art. Stark was not interested in elevating music—he was interested in selling it. After all, he was a businessman.

Joplin's interest in elevating ragtime to high art predated his move to St. Louis and his association with Ernst, who no doubt encouraged him in his hopes. This interest even predated the fame that came to Joplin following his success with "Maple Leaf Rag." Even before the rag had been released, he had been trying to think of a way to make ragtime respectable.

Joplin felt that if he worked hard enough, he could single-handedly elevate ragtime music not only for his own benefit but for the benefit of other black musicians. For ragtime was the music of much of black America. Joplin had decided that he would not limit his composing to the short piano rags he apparently could write with such ease. Several months before the Starks published "Maple Leaf Rag," he had started to compose the music for a larger work: a dramatic ragtime folk ballet. The form was his own creation, and it was a startling idea.

Joplin's ballet, called *The Ragtime Dance*, was based on black social dances of the era. He wrote the words

Joplin's note to ragtime players ("Do not play this piece fast. It is never right to play Ragtime fast.") began to appear on most of his sheet music after 1906.

TO PLAY RAGTIME IN EUROPE

An announcement in a 1901 edition of the St. Louis Post-Dispatch *announces what ultimately became Joplin's short-lived plans for a tour of Europe.*

and the music to the work and indicated which dances were to be performed. These included the ragtime dance, the cakewalk prance, the clean-up dance, the dude walk, the stop-time dance, the Jenny Cooler dance, the slow drag, and the back-step prance. The ballet consists of a vocal introduction, followed by the dances, which are directed by the vocalist. Joplin's associates and friends in Sedalia, including Arthur Marshall and Joplin's brother Will, encouraged him to work on *The Ragtime Dance* and helped him by copying out parts for the various instruments in the orchestra. Once the ballet was completed, Joplin formed the Scott Joplin Drama Company. In late 1899, he rented the Woods Opera House in Sedalia for a single performance—one performance of the ballet was all he could afford to produce. He invited everyone he knew, including the Stark family, whom he hoped could be persuaded to publish the lengthy work.

The performance was a success with Joplin's friends and acquaintances. But Stark was not interested in publishing it. He pointed out that the ballet was too long and too difficult to play. Besides, who would buy it? As a businessman, Stark understood the odds against such a work becoming popular. Yet Joplin felt that the publisher was being excessively cautious and was impeding his artistic development. Furthermore, the ballet was performed before the phenomenal success of "Maple Leaf Rag," so Joplin had not yet proved that his work would sell.

When Joplin moved to St. Louis, he continued to work on *The Ragtime Dance*. It is likely that he showed it to Ernst for his assessment. In late 1901, Joplin mounted another production of the ballet, this time solely for the Stark family. Stark's daughter Nell, who had recently returned from Europe, where she had been studying music, was in the audience. She enjoyed the ballet and tried to convince her father

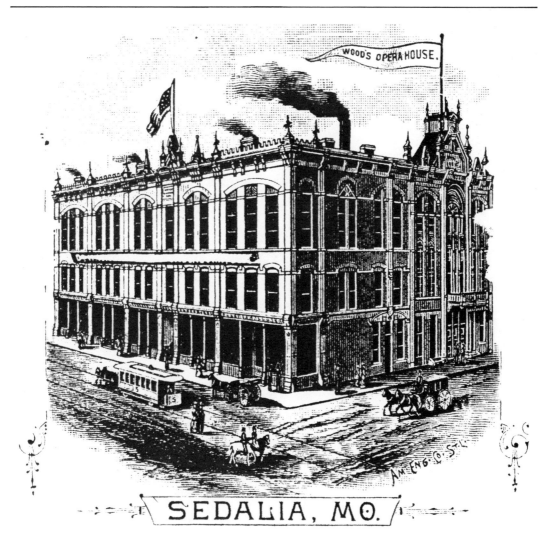

WOOD'S OPERA HOUSE.

SEDALIA, MO.

to publish it. However, Stark remained unenthusiastic about it. Angry at Stark's refusal to publish the ballet, Joplin decided to publish one of his rags, "The Easy Winners," on his own. The sheet music boasted on the cover: "Composed by Scott Joplin: King of Ragtime Writers." He also took several other rags to different publishers.

In 1902, Stark reluctantly gave in to Joplin's demands—perhaps because he felt he owed something to the composer. After all, "Maple Leaf Rag" had

Wood's Opera House in Sedalia was the site of the first performance of Joplin's folk ballet, The Ragtime Dance.

Although ragtime at the turn of the century was played chiefly by pianists, it was also performed by dance bands such as the New Orleans–based John Robichaux Orchestra (shown here).

made him a successful businessman. Ignoring his good business sense, Stark agreed to publish all nine pages of *The Ragtime Dance*.

Joplin was greatly encouraged. His compositions were selling well, and he believed that *The Ragtime Dance* would finally be recognized as a major work. An article in the Sedalia *Times* referred to him as the "Rag Time King," and the editor wrote that Joplin's compositions were "used by the leading players and orchestras." Furthermore, according to the article, he spent his time "writing, composing, and collecting his money from the different music houses in St. Louis, Chicago, New York and a number of other cities"—a rather enviable existence, although not quite an accurate description of Joplin's real life. The *St. Louis Globe-Democrat* also carried a biographical article. "Despite the ebony hue of his features and a retiring disposition," it reported, Joplin "has written probably more instrumental successes than any other local composer." The author also pointed out that Joplin was known as "The King of Rag Time Writers" because of "the many famous works in syncopated melodies which he has written."

Joplin and his wife soon moved to a larger apartment, where he started to work feverishly on yet another serious and large composition, a ragtime opera called *A Guest of Honor*. He continued to study with Ernst while teaching a fair number of his own students. His seriousness and devotion to music attracted a large number of pupils. They considered him a teacher, a mentor, and a hero. In retrospect, this is not surprising. Although Joplin was quiet, he was friendly and supportive, and he formed lasting friendships easily. In addition, he had a personality that many people found to be irresistible. Perhaps his quietness made the dynamic side of his personality seem all the more forceful. He possessed the will and the determination to make something of himself, to have his music and the music of his people accepted by American society. All of these personality traits earned him the respect of his peers along with the respect of the young musicians who sought to emulate him.

In March 1902, Joplin revived the Scott Joplin Drama Company and began to rehearse his opera. It was a one-act opera featuring 12 ragtime numbers. Marshall and Hayden were both members of the troupe, which Joplin soon decided to call "The Scott Joplin Ragtime Opera Company."

Following a series of rehearsals, *A Guest of Honor* was presented in a large dance hall in St. Louis, and the reaction of the audience was favorable. However, to Joplin's great disappointment, Stark was not interested in publishing the work. His business sense about *The Ragtime Dance* had been correct, and the ballet had not sold well. People wanted rags they could sing or play on their parlor pianos. They did not want to buy a ragtime ballet or opera. Stark was not at all interested in sinking more time and money into another large, serious musical work that the ragtime-buying public would ignore.

Despite his troubles with Stark, Joplin was fairly content. He was happy to be writing and teaching. However, his growing fame as "The Ragtime King" was beginning to be a problem. Because Joplin was the "King," he was challenged more often than ever before to play in ragtime competitions. In these contests, which were judged by the audience, two pianists would compete by playing faster and increasingly complex versions of the same tune. Although Joplin preferred to spend his time composing rather than playing, his many years spent as a performer—as well as his pride in his skill, ability, and experience—would not allow him to ignore these challenges.

However, ragtime performances had changed since Joplin had given up steady performing. The preferred performance style had become flashier, more demanding technically, and faster. Joplin's style of playing, like all of his rags, was still lyrical, slow, and serious. Determined to elevate ragtime into a more serious musical form, he was not interested in the flashy and less serious style of the newer rags. All of his rags had begun to appear with the instruction "Not Fast."

Consequently, Joplin's style of playing was not flashy or fast enough to impress the new ragtime audiences. His serious rags and his serious style of performing were no longer appreciated as much as they had been in earlier years. Accordingly, he began to play less often in public. He refused to play for people who were not interested in his style of music.

Joplin was also encountering troubles at home. His work on A Guest of Honor took up more and more of his time. And Belle, who did not understand his preoccupation with music, started to feel ignored and abandoned by him. Marshall later described the problems that the couple had by saying: "Mrs. Joplin wasn't so interested in music, and her taking violin lessons from Scott was a perfect failure. Mr. Joplin was seriously humiliated. Of course unpleasant attitudes and lack of home interests occurred between them. . . . [Joplin] told me his wife had no interest in his musical career." The family discord disturbed Joplin's concentration, and his work began to suffer, which must have made him even more impatient and irritable with Belle.

In late 1902, Belle announced that she was expecting a child. Both she and her husband were happy with this new development, hopeful that a baby would help to draw them back together. But their hopes were ill founded. The child, a girl, was born sickly and lived for only a few months. Belle became despondent after the baby's death, and she and Joplin decided in mid-1903 to separate. Joplin sold their home to Marshall, and then he moved in with the Turpins for a short while.

With the collapse of his marriage, Joplin also lost his concentration. The past months, which had been filled with anger, tension, and unhappiness, had left him upset. He had been on top of the world only a short time before. He had thought that his days of wandering were over. Now St. Louis was just a town full of bad memories. He decided to leave the area, and by the fall of 1903 he was on the road again.

The Chrysanthemum

AN AFRO-INTERMEZZO

BY

Scott Joplin.

PUBLISHED BY

JOHN STARK & SON.
St. Louis Mo.

5

6

AT LOOSE
ENDS

❦

AT LOOSE ENDS in the fall of 1903, Joplin remembered that the St. Louis production of *A Guest of Honor* had attracted the attention of two of the major booking agencies in town, Majestic and Haviland. Both of the agencies had been interested in promoting a touring production of the opera. Joplin promptly decided to take the Scott Joplin Ragtime Opera Company and *A Guest of Honor* on the road.

The company had 12 members when it left St. Louis in the fall of 1903. At first the tour went well. Joplin was received as a celebrity in the saloons and cafés of the small towns in the Midwest. There he was able to play his works in his own style; he was able to forget about the flashy and rapid-fire playing of the hotshot St. Louis performers. The company performed in Nebraska, Iowa, and Missouri, and may also have gone to Illinois and Kentucky. However, the tour started to run into troubles after a month on the road. Perhaps there were personality conflicts that arose between members of the company, or the composer was displeased for some reason with the performances. Or maybe the company simply did not make enough money to suit everyone. In any case, at least five members left the company after the first month of the tour. The remaining seven members pooled their abilities and past-performance experience and formed a minstrel show, which was booked

Published in 1904, "The Chrysanthemum" was subtitled by Joplin as "An Afro-Intermezzo," reflecting his interest in both Afro-American and classical music.

into various theaters and halls in Missouri, Nebraska, and Iowa in September and October. However, this company collapsed as well.

A discouraged Joplin prepared to return to St. Louis. When he arrived there, he was greeted with a parade. The residents of Chestnut Valley had apparently heard of his impending arrival and had decided that they were not going to let their favorite ragtime composer return to St. Louis feeling as though he was a failure. They hoped to show their support and lift his spirits with the parade. Despite this welcome, he stayed in St. Louis only briefly.

In early 1904, Joplin went back to Sedalia, the site of his early success. He listed himself in the town's directory as a musician, and he probably resumed his old work pattern of performing in the evening and composing during the day. Yet he was not any happier in Sedalia, so he soon packed his bags and moved back to St. Louis. Stark had also moved from Sedalia to St. Louis near the start of 1905. Thanks to Joplin's music, his publishing company was prospering and had outgrown its quarters in its hometown. Joplin maintained contact with Stark even though their five-year contract had expired and the composer was legally free to publish with whomever he pleased.

After Stark moved his firm to St. Louis, he started to show a glimmer of interest in publishing Joplin's opera. Perhaps he did not want to lose Joplin's business and his friendship. But although Stark expressed interest in acquiring *A Guest of Honor*, his firm never published it.

Joplin had applied for a copyright for the opera in early 1903, but no manuscript of the work was ever sent to the Copyright Office in Washington, D.C. All copies of the opera have subsequently been lost. Today, the whereabouts of *A Guest of Honor* continues to tantalize any scholar or music lover who has ever been interested in Scott Joplin.

During 1904, Joplin published four new rags and one song. "The Cascades—A Rag" was written to commemorate the beautiful Cascades Gardens, a huge complex of fountains, pools, lagoons, and ponds that served as the main concourse of the 1904 St. Louis Fair. Two other rags, "The Sycamore—A Concert Rag" and "The Chrysanthemum—An Afro-Intermezzo," reflect in their titles the classical influence that Joplin's teacher, Alfred Ernst, still had on him. They also reflect Joplin's continued determination to elevate ragtime to a higher status in the musical world.

Late in 1905, Joplin left St. Louis and went to Chicago, where he stayed with Marshall and his wife. Joplin also became reacquainted with several younger musicians whom he had known in the past. With Marshall as a collaborator, he wrote "The Lily Queen."

Ragtime performers from as far away as New Orleans came to the St. Louis World's Fair in 1904 to participate in piano-playing competitions as well as to earn money by playing for the crowds who attended the fair.

A talented yet highly undisciplined performer and composer, Louis Chauvin (shown here) never fulfilled the musical promise that many of his friends—including Joplin—expected of him.

And with the help of 23-year-old Louis Chauvin, a young friend from St. Louis and a student of Tom Turpin's, he wrote a work entitled "Heliotrope Bouquet."

Working with Chauvin was ultimately discouraging, for the younger musician represented the underside of life as an itinerant musician. Chauvin was only 17 when he had first met Joplin shortly after the composer and his wife moved to St. Louis. Chauvin quickly became a part of Joplin's circle of friends. It was obvious that he had talent and much promise as both a pianist and composer. Unfortunately, he was in love with the fast life of the red-light district and was unwilling to give it up. When Joplin met him in Chicago, Chauvin was paying the price for living a fast life. Addicted to opium, he was usually so high on the drug that he could not concentrate on what he was doing. Although he was blessed with the ability to write beautiful melodies, he did not have the concentration or the self-discipline to finish anything. Fragments of his melodies lay around his residence, written on scraps of paper.

Joplin was shocked and saddened when he saw what had become of Chauvin. He took two of the younger man's beautiful themes, added to them two of his own, and put them all together to make "Heliotrope Bouquet." Although Chauvin and Joplin worked together for a while on the piece, Joplin did most of the polishing, for Chauvin had difficulty concentrating on their work. "Heliotrope," an instrumental piece, was published by Stark in 1907—only a year before Louis Chauvin died from syphilis at the age of 24.

Chauvin's fate was not an unusual one for musicians whose principal places of employment were in the sporting districts of large cities. It was difficult to resist the dangerous temptations in such areas—difficult especially for a young and immature musi-

Like his friend Joplin, Arthur Marshall also published his rags—including "Ham and"—with John Stark & Son.

Although ragtime was usually performed by men, a number of women wrote rags. The most prominent of the female ragtime composers was May Aufderheide.

cian. The waste of Chauvin's talent reinforced Joplin's determination to make ragtime music respectable.

However, Joplin was continuing to find it difficult to concentrate. After staying with the Marshalls for a short while, he moved to a boarding house. But before long, in 1906, he left Chicago and resumed the life of a wandering performer. He traveled around the Midwest, playing wherever he was offered work. In 1907, he found himself back in the vicinity of his hometown of Texarkana, Texas. He decided to visit the members of his family who still lived there. His mother had died some years earlier, but his father was still in town, living with Scott's older brother, Monroe, and his family.

Joplin received a tumultuous welcome from the black community of Texarkana. He was a local boy who had overcome his impoverished beginnings and had become a success. His name was known all over the country, and his music could be found propped up on the pianos in most of the parlors in America. Joplin's homecoming was especially exciting for his family. They kept him up for most of the night after he arrived, talking and reminiscing. Long after midnight, Joplin played some of his pieces for his family on the piano. "I heard the music and I got out of bed and just sat there, listening," his nephew Fred Joplin recalled.

During Joplin's return to Texarkana, he taught his young niece Nettie how to play "Maple Leaf Rag." He also did some entertaining around town. After staying there for a few days, he went back to St. Louis, never to return to his Texas hometown.

Joplin settled down once more in St. Louis at a time when his rate of composition had fallen off drastically. He had published only three works in 1906, making it his least productive year since 1901. He must have been profoundly discouraged by this, for in 1907 he listed himself in the St. Louis directory as a laborer rather than a musician.

SCOTT JOPLIN.

It Was He Who Gave Us That Cleverest of Rags, "Maple Leaf"—Other Clever Numbers From His Pen.

The subject of this sketch, Scott Joplin, is a negro who is considered to be one of the greatest composers of ragtime music in this country. He gave us that clever and best of rags, "Maple Leaf," which has sold for years, and will sell for years to come.

One of his recent efforts is a march entitled "Antoinette," written in 6-8 time. It is an excellent composition and one that should become a favorite with bands and orchestras.

Scott Joplin has been working a considerable time on a grand opera which will contain music similar to that sung by the negroes during slavery days, the music of today, the negro ragtime, and the music that the negro will use in the future.

While in St. Louis the writer paid a visit to the John Stark Music Company, where he met and heard Mr. Joplin play the overture of his new opera, and to say that it was exceptionally good would be putting it mildly.

Scott Joplin considers it too hard work for him to sit at the piano and compose. He gets his inspirations while walking along the street or in his bed at night, and when a melody comes to him he immediately puts it down on music paper, which he always carries with him.

He is unassuming and never has much to say, and seldom speaks of his music. The Stark Music Company, of St. Louis, Mo., publishes his compositions.

This article about Joplin was originally published in a 1907 edition of a New York City music trade magazine.

One of the best-known white composers of ragtime, Joseph Lamb (center) had his pieces published by John Stark & Son.

In 1907, Joplin decided (perhaps in desperation) to visit John Stark, who had moved his offices from St. Louis to New York City. For years, Joplin had wanted to go to New York. This seemed to be as good a time in his life as any.

During the early 1900s, New York was starting to become one of the most heavily populated black urban areas in the United States. A large number of blacks were leaving the rural South for greater job opportunities in the industrial North. Among these migrants were black musicians and entertainers anxious to become a part of New York's growing black community.

At the time, there were more than 100 publishers in New York City competing with each other in the lucrative ragtime market. After arriving in New York, Joplin caught some of the sense of optimism that was in the air, and he started to perform and compose again. In 1907, he published eight different works— a large increase over his output just one year before.

Joplin soon signed up to tour on the vaudeville circuit. He spent the next several years on the road billed as "The King of Ragtime Composers—the Author of Maple Leaf Rag." During the tour, he performed in theaters and halls rather than in honky-tonks and saloons. He was also able to perform in his own slow and smooth style. He was still battling against the pianists who were primarily interested in playing ragtime as fast as they possibly could. They did not seem to care whether they were playing the right notes or rhythms. His serious attitude managed to show through in his performances. Instead of act-ing like a vaudeville performer, he presented the image of a serious musician.

During this tour, Joplin traveled all over the Mid-west and up and down the East Coast. On a visit to Washington, D.C., in 1907, he met 33-year-old Lot-tie Stokes. They fell in love and were soon married. Lottie began to travel with Joplin on his tours. Lottie's attitude toward his music was the opposite of Scott's first wife, Belle. Lottie loved his music and was en-thusiastic about all of his projects and dreams. In time, she would prove to be his fiercest defender and supporter. The love and support that Lottie gave Jop-lin meant a great deal to him. For the first time in years, he began to look to the future with confidence and anticipation. ❧

Overindulgent nightlife activities in the sporting districts inspired such works as "Stewed Chicken Rag."

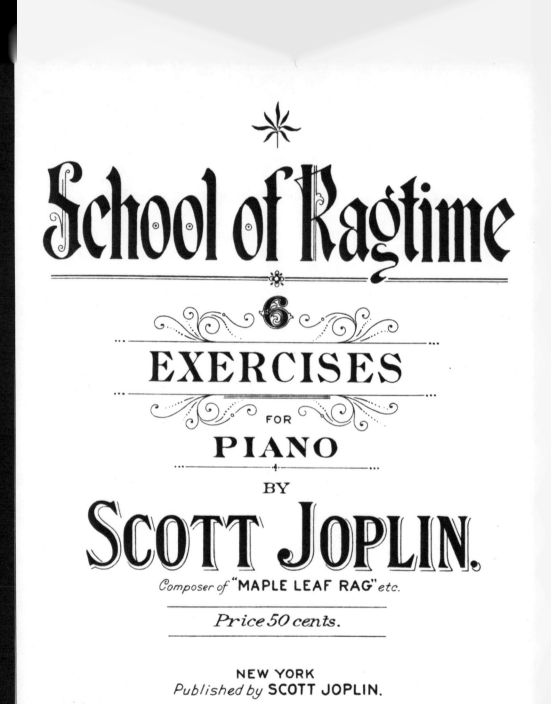

School of Ragtime

6 EXERCISES

FOR

PIANO

BY

SCOTT JOPLIN.

Composer of "MAPLE LEAF RAG" etc.

Price 50 cents.

NEW YORK
Published by SCOTT JOPLIN.

7

"NEVER
PLAY RAGTIME
FAST"

***

DURING THE FIRST decade of the 20th century, most of the well-crafted, high-quality rags were forced off the market by simpler, less interesting rags, which were published for a market that was looking for easy rags to play. Most amateur pianists did not recognize the difference between the commercialized rags printed by Tin Pan Alley publishers and the classic rags of Joplin and those who were influenced by him.

Joplin understood that an amateur pianist could have trouble playing his complicated rhythms. However, he believed that the solution to this difficulty was not to simplify the rags but to correctly train the pianists. To help their training, he wrote a ragtime instruction manual entitled *The School of Ragtime*. It consists of a set of six exercises designed to assist those amateur pianists who were having trouble with the complicated rhythms of ragtime. Originally published in 1908, *The School of Ragtime* was the first book on ragtime published by a black American. A ragtime instruction manual written by a white ragtime pianist had been published in 1897.

In his preface to *The School of Ragtime*, Joplin denounced the trashy commercial pieces that were "masquerading under the name of ragtime." These pieces, he wrote, were "not the genuine article." He also attacked the type of ragtime performance that

Published in 1908, The School of Ragtime *was written by Joplin to help pianists who wanted to master ragtime's complicated rhythms.*

Axel Christiansen opened up a nationwide chain of ragtime schools to teach people how to play ragtime music.

emphasized speed. In the directions to the first exercise in his book, Joplin wrote, "Never play ragtime fast at any time." By then, of course, these instructions had become something of a motto for him.

The controversy surrounding ragtime concerned more than just its often-frenzied performance style. It seemed to Joplin that the harder he struggled to have ragtime recognized by the musical establishment, the more difficult that struggle became. By 1910, the attacks on ragtime in newspapers, magazines, books, and pamphlets were coming faster and more furious than ever. With most of the classical musical establishment opposed to ragtime, it was a discouraging time for Joplin and other lovers of high-quality ragtime music.

There were several reasons for all of the opposition to ragtime. The first was the growing distinction between classical music and popular music. Many music educators believed that it was necessary to teach Americans how to listen to and perform higher forms of music. Because ragtime music was so incredibly popular, it represented a serious threat to the attempts of these classical music lovers to elevate the musical tastes of most Americans. As early as 1899, the music magazine *Etude* was warning:

> Pass along the streets of any large city of a summer evening when the windows are open and take note of what music you hear being played. It is no longer the great masters, or the lesser classicists—nor even the "Salon-componisten" that used to be prime favorites with the boarding-school misses. Not a bit of it! It is "rag-time."

Ragtime was described in magazine articles as a "ragweed of music" and "a poison that destroys the musical tastes of the young." One writer in 1901 sputtered with indignation that "this cheap, trashy stuff could not elevate even the most degraded minds,

While Joplin was producing some of his best-known rags, composer Charles Ives (shown here) wrote innovative classical pieces that often made use of American folk music.

nor could it possibly urge any one to greater effort in the acquisition of culture in any phase." A writer in the *Negro Music Journal* of 1902 sought to rally the antiragtime troops by saying: "Let us take a united stand against the *Ragtime Evil* as we would against bad literature, and horrors of war or intemperance and other socially destructive evils."

In addition to the highbrows who were concerned with musical taste, there were also many people who were deeply concerned with decaying morals, especially of the young. These individuals were quick to point out that ragtime had originated in honky-tonks, saloons, and other places of ill repute. It was obvious, they argued, that any musical style with its origins in such places had to be bad, even if it was played on a parlor piano. They believed that ragtime would inevitably lower moral standards. These same opponents of ragtime also decided that because it was so popular, it must be addictive or have unknown, mysterious powers. *Etude* in 1900 called ragtime a "virulent poison" and pointed out that it was "finding its way into the homes and the brains of the youth to such an extent as to arouse one's suspicions of their sanity." Others claimed that ragtime's extensive use of syncopation would cause permanent brain damage and harm the nervous systems of listeners and performers.

Much of the moral criticism of ragtime and many of the suspicions about it and its origins were, in fact, poorly disguised excuses for racism. America was a highly segregated society, and many white Americans felt threatened by this musical form because it not only had been developed by black Americans but also because it incorporated strong elements of African and Afro-American rhythms. Ragtime opponents believed that the words to ragtime songs, the melodies of ragtime pieces, and the unconventional ragtime rhythms were indecent.

Joplin's fight to legitimize ragtime was, to a large extent, a fight to legitimize the music of black Americans. It is easy to see how he might have become discouraged by the situation. But even though his dream of turning ragtime into a respected art form sometimes seemed to be an impossible one, he refused to give up. As Stark had discovered when Joplin tried to get him to publish *The Ragtime Dance*, Joplin could be a very stubborn man. He refused to simplify his rags and write instead pieces that were easy to play. In fact, after 1905, he almost always included the following instruction in the left-hand corner of his composition: "*NOTICE!*: Do not play this piece fast. It is never right to play ragtime fast. The Composer."

In his continuing struggle, Joplin had one staunch supporter: John Stark. After settling in New York City, Stark had refused to publish the unrefined yet popular commercial pieces that other publishers were

A longtime supporter of serious ragtime music, John Stark was unwilling to publish the slick, commercially successful rags that were being issued by most other music publishers in the early 1900s.

Admirers of classical music criticized the black-inspired music of ragtime for a variety of reasons. Some of these criticisms were racially motivated.

turning out daily. He remained loyal to Joplin and his serious and artistic rags. Stark even paid for large advertisements in the musical press to support serious ragtime, and he sometimes ridiculed the antiragtime snobbery of those who promoted classical music. His advertisement for Joplin's "The Cascades" is a good example of his advertising campaign. Stark wrote

A FIERCE TRAGEDY IN ONE ACT

SCENE: A Fashionable Theatre. Enter Mrs. Van Clausenberg and party—late, of course.

MRS. VAN C.: "What is the orchestra playing? It is the grandest thing I have ever heard. It is positively inspiring."

YOUNG AMERICA (in the seat behind): "Why, that is the 'Cascades' by Joplin."

MRS. VAN C.: "Well, that is one on me. I thought I had heard all of the great music, but this is the most thrilling piece I have ever heard. I suppose Joplin is a Pole who was educated in Paris."

YOUNG AM: "Not so you could notice it. He's a young Negro from Texarkana, and the piece they are playing is a rag."

Sensation—Perturbation—Trepidation—and Seven Other Kinds of Emotion.

MRS. VAN C.: "#%&*$@ The idea! The very word ragtime rasps my finer sensibilities. (Rising) I'm going home and I'll never come to this theatre again. I just can't stand trashy music."

Yet Stark's loyalty to Joplin had a price. Stark's faith in serious ragtime caused him financial difficulties. The Tin Pan Alley publishers had begun to consolidate into larger companies, which then reduced the price of their music, undercutting their competition. Stark was caught in a bind. Not only were the rags that he published not as popular as the others, but he also had to charge more for them. He began to lose business fast. And to make matters worse, his wife became seriously ill.

In response to highbrow criticisms of ragtime, John Stark used this advertisement to poke fun at the classical music establishment.

To improve his financial situation, Stark suggested to Joplin in 1909 that on future compositions they give up the royalty arrangement they had always used in the past. Stark suggested that he would instead purchase the composer's pieces outright for a specific sum of money. Joplin was outraged at this suggestion. He considered Stark's plan to be an insult, and he refused. Joplin argued that publishers usually purchased pieces outright only from struggling young composers—not from composers who were as well known and as well established as he was. Stark, in turn, became angry with Joplin, for he believed that Joplin owed him something for his years of loyalty.

Stark told Joplin that he would never again publish any of his works. The long-standing and mutually beneficial association that had existed between Joplin and Stark for more than 10 years came to an end.

Over the years, Joplin had become increasingly convinced that there was only one way for him to win the support and respect of the established music community, which seemed prepared to condemn all forms of ragtime—even Joplin's serious classical rags. He had never given up on his dream of producing a successful large-scale musical work. He had been discouraged by his inability to get *A Guest of Honor* published. However, he still believed that a large-scale work was the correct route to acceptance. It was up to him to write a work of such stellar quality that the musical establishment would be forced to sit up and take notice.

Back when Joplin was living in St. Louis, he had started to work on another large musical composition in addition to *A Guest of Honor*. He had continued to work on the composition off and on for several years. His life on the vaudeville circuit greatly interrupted his composing, making it almost impossible for him to find long stretches of uninterrupted time in which to write. After he married Lottie, he wanted to settle in one place. It had been almost five years since he had lived in a real home. But he had no savings, and very little money was coming in from publishers in the form of royalty fees.

By 1907, he had completed enough of the large-scale work to be able to play parts of it for friends in Washington, D.C. By 1908, he had a finished draft. He would continue to work on the composition for the last 10 years of his life. It would be the source of much pain, frustration, and disappointment for him, but it would also be, according to many, the crowning achievement of his life. The composition was his second opera, *Treemonisha*. ◄◊►

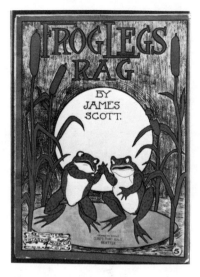

Ragtime composer James Scott received a tremendous boost in his career when Joplin recommended to John Stark that he publish Scott's "Frog Legs Rag."

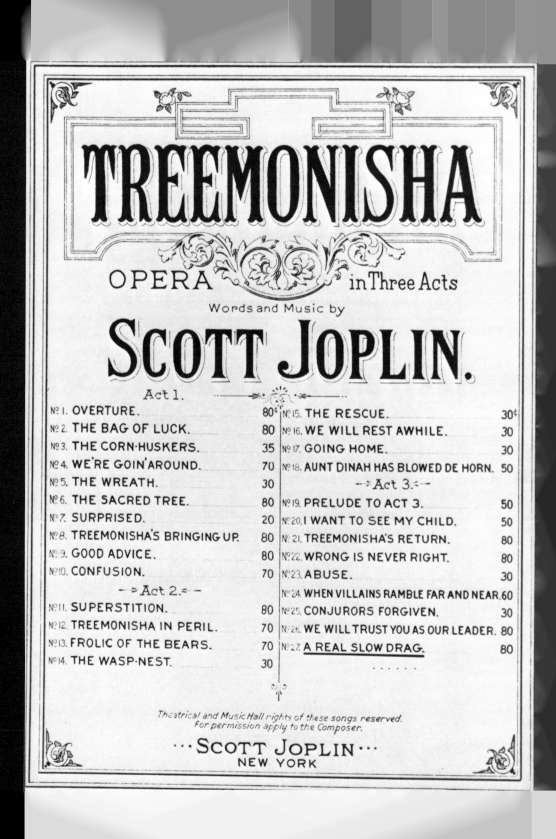

TREEMONISHA

OPERA in Three Acts

Words and Music by

SCOTT JOPLIN.

Act 1.

Nº 1. OVERTURE.	80¢	
Nº 2. THE BAG OF LUCK.	80	
Nº 3. THE CORN-HUSKERS.	35	
Nº 4. WE'RE GOIN' AROUND.	70	
Nº 5. THE WREATH.	30	
Nº 6. THE SACRED TREE.	80	
Nº 7. SURPRISED.	20	
Nº 8. TREEMONISHA'S BRINGING UP.	80	
Nº 9. GOOD ADVICE.	80	
Nº 10. CONFUSION.	70	

Act 2.

Nº 11. SUPERSTITION.	80
Nº 12. TREEMONISHA IN PERIL.	70
Nº 13. FROLIC OF THE BEARS.	70
Nº 14. THE WASP-NEST.	30

Nº 15. THE RESCUE.	30¢
Nº 16. WE WILL REST AWHILE.	30
Nº 17. GOING HOME.	30
Nº 18. AUNT DINAH HAS BLOWED DE HORN.	50

Act 3.

Nº 19. PRELUDE TO ACT 3.	50
Nº 20. I WANT TO SEE MY CHILD.	50
Nº 21. TREEMONISHA'S RETURN.	80
Nº 22. WRONG IS NEVER RIGHT.	80
Nº 23. ABUSE.	30
Nº 24. WHEN VILLAINS RAMBLE FAR AND NEAR.	60
Nº 25. CONJURORS FORGIVEN.	30
Nº 26. WE WILL TRUST YOU AS OUR LEADER.	80
Nº 27. A REAL SLOW DRAG.	80

. . . .

Theatrical and Music Hall rights of these songs reserved.
For permission apply to the Composer.

··· SCOTT JOPLIN ···
NEW YORK

8

DOWNBEAT

O UT OF ECONOMIC necessity, Joplin continued to travel and perform during 1910. Despite the distractions and disruptions of his hectic schedule, he managed to finish a second draft of *Treemonisha* by the end of the year. The following year, he and his wife rented some rooms in a boarding house on West 47th Street in New York. Joplin gave up performing on the vaudeville circuit and instead earned a living by teaching a few students. However, most of his time and energy went to work on the opera. He had almost completely given up writing ragtime piano pieces; in 1910, he published only two works, and he would publish only one ragtime piece in 1911 and one in 1912.

There was no extra money in the Joplin household, but there was friendship and good times. Their home on 47th Street was located in an area of New York where numerous musicians and actors lived. The Joplin rooms were often filled with people who were also entertainers.

Located just a block from Broadway, the main street in New York's theater district, the Joplin home was also in the middle of the Tin Pan Alley area. The nearby streets were lined with the shops of music publishers. Once Joplin felt that he was more or less finished with his opera, he attempted to find a publisher for it. Day after day, he went from firm to firm

Published in 1911, Treemonisha is an opera in three acts. Although the opera contains 27 musical numbers, only 3 of them are pure rags.

91

One of the last works to be published by John Stark, "Felicity Rag" was the only piece of ragtime music to be issued by Joplin in 1911, the same year that he finished working on Treemonisha.

with the manuscript of the opera in hand. No one was the least bit interested in publishing it. Although Joplin became discouraged, he was determined that *Treemonisha* would not suffer the same fate as had *A Guest of Honor*.

After months of rejection, Joplin decided to give up on the New York publishers and publish *Treemonisha* himself. He somehow managed to scrape together enough money to pay for a printer. The manuscript first appeared in May 1911, under his own imprint: Scott Joplin Music Pub. Co., New York City, N.Y.

The score to *Treemonisha* is 230 pages long. The work is a grand opera in three acts, complete with an orchestral overture and instrumental preludes to the second and third acts. There are 27 musical numbers in the opera, including recitatives (sung dialogue), arias (songs), and choruses. There are also several dances, to which Joplin choreographed the dance steps himself. In *Treemonisha*, he synthesized all the ragtime forms he had developed over the years. In some of the pieces, he integrated the rag style in a subtle fashion. However, the overall work is not a ragtime opera, for only three of the numbers are obviously and unmistakably ragtime in style. In fact, Joplin called *Treemonisha* a folk opera.

The opera's plot is rather simple, but the underlying message is one that had been of vital importance to Joplin for most of his life. The story is set in Texarkana, Texas, between 1866 and 1884. The main characters—all blacks—are former slaves who have been left to fend for themselves in the woods of eastern Texas after the Civil War. They are simple people who live in ignorance and believe in superstition and conjuring. Because of their superstitions, it has been easy for conjurers to cheat them out of their money by selling them "bags of luck."

Joplin in 1911, around the time when he and his second wife, Lottie, were living in the part of New York City known as Tin Pan Alley.

Treemonisha is the main character in the opera. Her mother's name is Monisha, and as a child the girl loved to sit under a particular tree—hence her name, Treemonisha. Her parents arrange for her to be educated, and the opera commences when Treemonisha is 18 and has just started her career as a teacher and leader of her people. The plot revolves around the conflict between Treemonisha and the neighborhood conjurer, who understands that once the people are no longer superstitious, he will lose his livelihood. By the end of the opera, Treemonisha outsmarts the conjurer, and knowledge triumphs over ignorance. The opera's message—that education is the salvation of black people in the United States—was close to Joplin's heart.

Soon after Joplin published the opera, a rave review appeared in the June 1911 issue of *American Musician*, praising him as "a teacher as well as a scholar and an optimist with a mission. . . . [He] has created an original type of music in which he employs syncopation in a most artistic and original manner. . . . Moreover, he has created an entirely new phase of musical art and has produced a thoroughly American opera." These kind words helped Joplin to feel as though his music had finally been recognized for what it was: original, artistic, and truly American.

Armed with copies of the review, Joplin set off in search of backers for a production of *Treemonisha*. He placed notices in local newspapers and knocked on the doors of dozens of potential producers. The lack of interest was disappointing. However, in August 1913, a notice appeared in *New York Age* announcing that the opera would be produced that fall at the Lafayette Theatre in Harlem. Joplin was overjoyed and immediately advertised for singers. But the production soon fell through, and Joplin fell into a deep depression.

In late 1913, Joplin managed to pull himself out of his depression and wrote one of his last rags, "Magnetic Rag." He was low on money and hoped to earn some income from the royalties. He also advertised for more students. To save rent money, he and Lottie moved from 47th Street to a building on West 138th Street in the district known as Harlem, which was quickly becoming one of the most heavily populated black areas in New York.

Sam Patterson, an old friend and former student of Joplin's from St. Louis, arrived in New York at around this time and volunteered to help the composer with his opera. The instrumental part of *Treemonisha* had been written for the piano only; Joplin

When Treemonisha was first performed in 1915, it generated little enthusiasm. However, when the opera opened in New York City's theater district 60 years later (in the production advertised here), it became a Pulitzer Prize-winning success.

Jelly Roll Morton became a popular jazz pianist after drawing upon his musical roots in the sporting clubs of New Orleans, where he often heard ragtime being played.

had planned to stage a performance of the opera himself with the hope of attracting backers. It was a tremendous job to transform the music for the piano into music for various instruments of the orchestra. The two worked day and night on the orchestration.

In early 1915, Joplin rented the Lincoln Theatre on 135th Street in Harlem for a performance of *Treemonisha.* He gathered together a group of singers and dancers who probably worked for little or no pay. Joplin worked hard at rehearsing the cast and hammering the opera into shape. However, despite all of the long hours that he and Patterson had put into orchestrating the opera, it soon became apparent that there was no money to hire an orchestra. At the first performance of *Treemonisha,* Joplin himself ended up playing all of the music on the piano. Likewise, there was no money for costumes or scenery, so the production was rather bleak. Confident of the power of his music, Joplin hoped that the opera would succeed on the basis of the music and the dancing.

He was wrong. The audience, which consisted mostly of friends, was small. Their applause was polite but not enthusiastic. The lukewarm reception was not what Joplin had hoped to hear.

Even if *Treemonisha* had been mounted splendidly, complete with costumes, scenery, and a full orchestra, it probably would not have succeeded. The opera's subject matter was too close to home for many black Americans in 1915. They did not want to be reminded of life on plantations in the South, where

King Oliver's Creole Band, based in New Orleans and featuring musician Louis Armstrong (kneeling in front), became one of the first groups in the country to play jazz.

A band plays Joplin's ''Maple Leaf Rag'' at his grave site in New York during a recent memorial service.

ignorance and superstition were commonplace. They were anxious to put their unpleasant history behind them.

Even worse than the polite reaction of the audience was that of the musical press: virtual silence.

For Joplin, the failure of *Treemonisha* meant the end of a life's worth of dreams and hopes. He had been in failing health for some time, but his obsession with the opera had given him the strength to press on and to ignore his physical problems. The opera's failure was a blow from which he would not recover.

Joplin not only fell into a deep depression, but he began to exhibit increasingly erratic behavior. His mood would swing suddenly from elation to lethargy. He did not play the piano anymore. He could not even remember his own compositions. Much like his friend Louis Chauvin, he was unable to concentrate. He began to stumble over words, and his handwriting deteriorated.

By late 1916, Joplin started to act somewhat paranoid. He began to think that people were stealing music from him. Near the start of 1917, he destroyed many of the musical sketches and unfinished pieces that were on his desk. He still had lucid periods, but they were becoming less and less frequent.

On February 5, 1917, Joplin was admitted to the Manhattan State Hospital. He soon became paralyzed and could not even recognize the friends who came to visit him. The March 29 issue of *New York Age* contained the following notice: "Scott Joplin, composer of the Maple Leaf Rag and other syncopated melodies, is a patient at Ward's Island for mental trouble." Three days later, on April 1, 1917, he died at the age of 48. The cause of his death was "dementia paralytica-cerebral," with contributing complications from syphilis, although his wife would later say of him, "You might say he died of disappointment, his health broken mentally and physically."

A funeral for Joplin was held on April 5, 1917. He was buried in a common grave in St. Michael's Cemetery on Long Island, New York. Joplin had made a request years before that "Maple Leaf Rag" be played at his funeral. However, when Lottie was making the funeral arrangements, she decided that it would not be appropriate to play that particular work at a funeral. Yet she later regretted this decision, saying, "How many, many times since then I've wished to my heart that I'd said yes."

Ragtime did not die with Joplin in 1917, but it almost did. Its incredible popularity in the first years of this century soon faded. The fickle American public embraced it for a short time, then forgot it.

In fact, by the time of Joplin's death, ragtime was already losing its popularity. Rags were still published on occasion, but the incredible interest in ragtime had run its course. By the time that Joplin's friend Tom Turpin died in 1922, the days of ragtime were finished. The American public, in the days of the Roaring Twenties, had a new musical style to call its own: jazz.

A generation after Joplin's death, both ragtime music and the name of Scott Joplin were almost totally unknown to most Americans. A handful of people, such as his wife and an old friend, S. Brunson Campbell, tried to promote ragtime. But their efforts, for the most part, were unsuccessful.

Over the years, this began to change. In 1945, a magazine called *The Record Changer* published a number of articles on Joplin. In the 1950s, books on ragtime began to appear.

By the 1960s, interest in ragtime had grown stronger. A magazine called *Rag Times*, featuring the motto "Scott Joplin Lives!", was founded in California in 1966. Soon afterward, a pianist and music historian named Joshua Rifkin, who was studying ragtime as a forerunner of jazz, realized that ragtime compositions were very interesting in themselves. In 1970, he released a ragtime recording that immediately became a hit.

In the mid-1970s, the name *Scott Joplin* and the word *ragtime* finally became widely known throughout America. George Roy Hill, a Hollywood film director, heard one of Rifkin's ragtime recordings and decided that ragtime music would serve as an ideal soundtrack for the movie he was making. The movie was *The Sting*, starring Robert Redford and Paul Newman.

Hill and composer Marvin Hamlisch selected a number of Joplin's rags—including "Gladiolus Rag,"

Actors Paul Newman (left) and Robert Redford starring in The Sting, *which won the 1974 Academy Award for Best Picture. The film's soundtrack, which featured Joplin's rags, won an Oscar as well and introduced ragtime to a new generation of listeners.*

Conductor Gunther Schuller and the New England Conservatory prepare to make a recording of Joplin's rags.

"Pine Apple Rag," "Solace," "The Ragtime Dance," and "The Entertainer"—to use in the soundtrack. Not only did *The Sting* go on to win the Academy Award for Best Picture in 1974, but both the soundtrack and the title song ("The Entertainer," renamed "The Sting") also won Oscars. By the fall of 1974, the soundtrack recording of *The Sting* had sold over two million copies. America was once again listening to Joplin's music.

Official recognition for Joplin soon followed. The residents of Sedalia started a Scott Joplin Memorial

Foundation, and a memorial plaque was erected on the site of the old Maple Leaf Club in honor of both Joplin and Stark. The people of Texarkana held a Scott Joplin Centennial Concert, during which his rags were played and members of his family were honored.

And *Treemonisha* was finally produced—first in Atlanta, next in Washington, D.C., and then in Houston, Texas. In 1975, a dream of Joplin's came true: *Treemonisha* opened before a packed audience on Broadway in New York. The crowd loved it.

A year later, Joplin was posthumously awarded a Pulitzer Prize. The prize was officially awarded for his opera, but in effect it was given to honor his lifetime of work as a composer of ragtime music. Joplin once commented that his music would not be appreciated until 50 years after his death. His estimation was not wrong by very much.

Joplin was a man who knew what he wanted and who was willing to work hard to fulfill his dreams. Lottie Joplin said of him, "He was a great man, a *great* man! He wanted to be a real leader. He wanted to free his people from poverty, ignorance, and su-perstition, just like the heroine of his ragtime opera, *Treemonisha*. That's why he was so ambitious; that's why he tackled major projects. In fact, that's why he was so far ahead of his time."

Today Scott Joplin's place in the history of American music is secure—thanks to his foresight, musical genius, and simple hard work. ❦

APPENDIX

COMPOSITIONS BY SCOTT JOPLIN

1895   "A Picture of Her Face"; "Please Say You Will"

1896   "Combination March"; "The Great Crush Collision March"; "Harmony Club Waltz"

1899   "Maple Leaf Rag"; "Original Rags" (arranged by Charles N. Daniels)

1900   "Swipesy—Cake Walk"

1901   "Augustan Club Waltz"; "Easy Winners"; "Peacherine Rag"; "Sunflower Slow Drag"

1902   "A Breeze from Alabama"; "Cleopha"; "Elite Syncopations"; "The Entertainer"; "I am Thinking of my Pickaninny Days"; "March Majestic"; "The Ragtime Dance"; "The Strenuous Life"

1903   "Little Black Baby"; "Palm Leaf Rag"; "Something Doing"; "Weeping Willow"; "A Guest of Honor"

1904   "The Cascades"; "The Sycamore"; "The Chrysanthemum"; "Maple Leaf Rag" (words by Sydney Brown); "The Favorite"

1905   "Bethena"; "Rosebud"; "Bink's Waltz"; "Leola"; "Sarah Dear" (words by Henry Jackson)

1906   "Antoinette"; "Ragtime Dance"; "Eugenia"

1907   "Gladiolus Rag"; "Lily Queen"; "Heliotrope Bouquet" (with Louis Chauvin); "The Nonpariel"; "Roseleaf Rag"; "Searchlight Rag"; "Snoring Sampson" (by Harry La Mertha; arranged by Scott Joplin); "When Your Hair Is Like the Snow" (words by Owen Spendthrift)

1908   "Fig Leaf Rag"; "Pine Apple Rag"; "School of Ragtime—6 Exercises for Piano"; "Sensation" (by Joseph F. Lamb; arranged by Scott Joplin); "Sugar Cane"

1909   "Country Club"; "Paragon Rag"; "Euphoric Sounds"; "Pleasant Moments"; "Solace"; "Wall Street Rag"

1910   "Pine Apple Rag" (words by Joe Snyder); "Stoptime Rag"

1911	"Felicity Rag"; "Prelude to Act Three" (*Treemonisha* excerpt); *Treemonisha*
1912	"Scott Joplin's New Rag"
1913	"Kismet Rag" (with Scott Hayden); "A Real Slow Drag" (*Treemonisha* excerpt)
1914	"Magnetic Rag"
1915	"Frolic of the Bears" (*Treemonisha* excerpt)
1917	"Reflection Rag"
1971	"Silver Swan Rag" (attributed to Scott Joplin)

CHRONOLOGY

Nov. 24, 1868	Born Scott Joplin in eastern Texas
1884	Forms Texas Melody Quartette
1888	Leaves home in Texarkana, Arkansas
1890	Arrives in St. Louis, Missouri
1893	Visits World Columbian Expedition in Chicago, Illinois
1895	Returns to St. Louis; tours with Texas Melody Quartette; first two songs, "Please Say You Will" and "A Picture of Her Face," are published
1897	Moves to Sedalia, Missouri; enters the Smith College of Music; the first piece of ragtime music is published
1898	Maple Leaf Club is founded in Sedalia
1899	"Original Rags" is published; forms Scott Joplin Drama Company; "Maple Leaf Rag" is published
1900	Marries Belle Hayden; meets Alfred Ernst
1901	Moves to St. Louis; becomes Ernst's pupil
1902	"The Entertainer" is published; completes A Guest of Honor; The Ragtime Dance is published
1903	Separates from his wife, Belle
1904	Returns to Sedalia
1905	Moves to St. Louis, then to Chicago
1907	Visits Texarkana; moves to New York; tours on vaudeville circuit; marries Lottie Stokes
1908	The School of Ragtime is published
1911	Treemonisha is published
1917	Enters Manhattan State Hospital in New York
April 1, 1917	Dies in New York

FURTHER READING

Berlin, Edward A. *Ragtime: A Musical and Cultural History.* Berkeley: University of California Press, 1980.

Blesh, Rudi, and Harriet Janis. *They All Played Ragtime.* ed. New York: Oak Publications, 1971.

Campbell, S. Brunson, and R. J. Carew. "Sedalia . . . Missouri, Cradle of Ragtime." *The Record Changer*, May 1945, pp. 3, 5, 25; June 1945, pp. 36–37.

———. "The Ragtime Kid (An Autobiography)." *Jazz Report* (June 1, 1967), n.p.

Carew, R. J. "Scott Joplin, Overlooked Genius." *The Record Changer*, September 1944, p. 12; October, 1944, p. 11–12.

Haskins, James, and Kathleen Benson. *Scott Joplin.* Garden City, New York: Doubleday, 1978.

Leonard, Neil. "The Reactions to Ragtime." In John Edward Hasse, ed., *Ragtime: Its History, Composers, and Music.* New York: Schirmer Books, 1985, pp. 102–113.

Reed, Addison W. "Scott Joplin, Pioneer." In John Edward Hasse, ed., *Ragtime: Its History, Composers, and Music.* New York: Schirmer Books, 1985, pp. 117–136.

Thompson, Kay C. "Lottie Joplin." *The Record Changer*, October, 1950, pp. 8, 18.

Vanderlee, Ann and John. "Scott Joplin's Childhood Days in Texas." *Rag Times*, November 1973, p. 5.

INDEX

———— ❧ ————

PICTURE CREDITS

———————— ❦ ————————

KATHERINE PRESTON is a music historian who lives near Washington, D.C. She is interested in all aspects of the history of music in American life, especially during the 19th century. As a free-lance writer, she has worked for the Library of Congress and the Smithsonian Institution, and her articles and reviews have appeared in *American Music, Popular Music,* and *The New Grove Dictionary of American Music.* She is currently working on a Ph.D. in musicology at the City University of New York.

NATHAN IRVIN HUGGINS is W.E.B. Du Bois Professor of History and Director of the W.E.B. Du Bois Institute for Afro-American Research at Harvard University. He previously taught at Columbia University. Professor Huggins is the author of numerous books, including *Black Odyssey: The Afro-American Ordeal in Slavery, The Harlem Renaissance,* and *Slave and Citizen: The Life of Frederick Douglass.*